CW00920100

Arabic Cooking

Step by Step

Lebanese Touch

First published in Beirut, Lebanon in 1997
by Arab Scientific Publishers

الدارالعـربـيــة للعـــلُوُم
Arab Scientific Publishers

Lina Bassam Chebaro
Nada Mosbah Halawani

Editing:
Lina Bassam Chebaro
Ghada Yamout Ramadan
Jamila Dandan
Nicole Awad

Food Preparation & Garnishing
Goodies Cuisine

Photoghraphy
Photo Naji

Desktop Publishing:
Abjad Graphics

Printing:
Mediterranean Press

الدارالعـربـيــة للعـــلُوُم
Arab Scientific Publishers

Reem Bldg., Sakiat Al-Janzir, Ain Al-Tenah, P.O.Box: 13/5574 - Beirut-Lebanon
Tel/Fax: 811373 - 860138 - 786233 - 785107 - 786607

Goodies

Arabic Cooking

Lebanese Touch

Step by Step

Contents

Arabic Cooking
Step by Step

 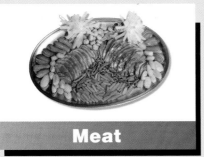

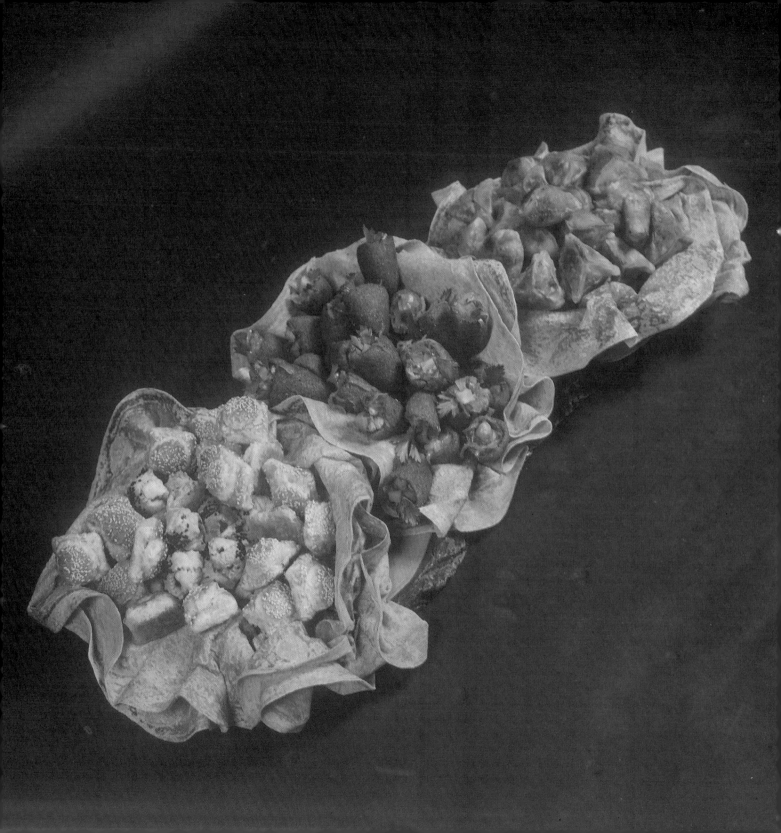

Introduction

For thousands of years, the Middle East has played a siginficant part in history as a trading link between East and West. Its dishes have been developed through the wide variety of foods carried by the caravans and diversity of societies encountered through trade.

Using this book, you can become an Arabic Chef, and taste the splendors and richness of the Arabic cuisine! Also, discover more than 170, step-by-step recipes each with a ready.made photo. The recipes have been prepared in cooperation with the famous Lebanese caterers "Goodies". This book includes 12 sections on salads, appetizers, pastries , soups, rice, grains, vegetables, chicken, meat, fish, pickles, and beverages; plus detailed basics, glossary and easy to use help. More than 500 photographs are included providing the user with all the information he or she needs. Moreover, pictures describing the harder-to-prepare recipes, like pastries, kibbi balls, and stuffed vine leaves is included.

Lina Chebaro

NB. "Arab Cooking" multimedia CD version in Arabic, English & French languages plus 25 minutes of video is available from the publishers.

BASICS

Boiling Dry Beans

1) Brown Lentils: Cook brown lentils covered with water for 1 hour and a half.
2) Red Lentils: Cook covered with water for 1 hour.
3) White Lentils: Cook covered with water for 15 minutes.
4) Chickpeas: Pre-soak in cold water for one night. In the morning, rinse well then drain. Place in a bowl covered with water. Stir in a dash of bicarbonate of soda. Place aside for 30 minutes. Pour chickpeas and water into a pot (add water if necessary). Bring to a boil on high heat. Add 1 cup of cold water, lower heat, and cook for 1 hour or until tender.

Note: You can use half cooked chickpeas in Mougrabiyah and Burghul Bil Dapheen.
5) Fava Beans (small or broad): Remove any impurities such as small stones or fibers. Presoak in water with a dash of bicarbonate of soda for 24 hours. Rinse well. Put fava beans covered with water in a pot. Bring to a boil on high heat. Add 1 cup water, lower heat, and cook for 1 hour or until tender.
6) Lima Beans (broad or small): Presoak covered with water for 1 night. Rinse well. Cook in double its amount of water for 20 minutes. Remove and drain.

Pressure-Cooker

A lidded saucepan made of thick aluminium in which food is cooked under pressure.
Both the base and the lid of the cooker have sturdy handles and the lid has a pressure gauge and a safety valve. Food is cooked quickly, thus saving time and fuel. Manufacturer's instructions should always be read carefully before using a pressure cooker.

Pressure Cooking:

Cooking is by means of pressure produced by steam from water within a pressure cooker. The major advantages of this method are speed, fuel economy and flavor retention as no steam escapes from the hermetically-sealed cooker.
Example: Stew meat: 2 hours in a normal pot
30-40 minutes in a pressure-cooker

Rice

Perfect Rice

Serves: 3
Makes: 3 cups
Preparation time: 10 minutes
Cooking time: about 30 minutes

Ingredients:

1 cup short-, medium, or long-grain rice
2 tablespoons unsalted butter, or 1 tablespoon vegetable oil or olive oil
1 1/2 cups homemade stock, or water
salt
2 tablespoons vermicelli

Steps:

1) Heat 1 tablespoon of the butter or oil in a heavy saucepan over medium-high heat. Add drained rice and gently sauté until all the grains are well coated, about 2 minutes.
2) Add stock or water and salt to taste. Bring to a boil, then stir once, reduce the heat to very low, cover tightly, and simmer rice for

17 minutes. Do not remove the cover or stir during cooking.
3) Remove rice from heat. If any liquid remains in the pot, cover again and place over low heat until the liquid evaporates, 2 to 4 minutes. Add remaining butter, if using, to the finished rice and fluff with a fork, lifting from the bottom instead of stirring, to separate grains gently.

Brown Rice

Serves: 4
Preparation / Cooking time: 40 minutes

Ingredients:

2 cups long grain rice
1 small finely chopped onion
1/2 cup canned and chopped mushroom (optional)
1 teaspoon sugar
1 teaspoon salt (as desired)
2 tablespoons shortening or butter
4 cups water

Steps:

First Way:

1) Fry chopped onion in butter until golden-brown.
2) Place sugar in a pot. Stir over moderate heat until brown.
3) Add water and fried onion to sugar. Cook over moderate heat for 10 minutes.
4) Add rice. Lower heat and continue cooking for 20 minutes.
5) Add mushroom. Cook for 5 minutes.
6) Serve rice accompanied with stews and meat dishes.

Second Way:

1) Fry onion with butter until golden-brown.
2) Add water. Bring to a boil for 10 minutes. Drain.
3) Cook rice with strained water.

Sauces

Garlic purée:

First Way:
Makes: 1 cup
Preparation time: 10 minutes

Ingredients:
1/4 cup lemon juice
1/2 cup olive oil
1 head of garlic, peeled and crushed
1/2 teaspoon salt

Steps:
1) Process crushed garlic with oil, lemon juice, and salt until smooth and thick.
2) Pour in bowls and serve next to meat and chicken.

Second Way:
Makes: 1 cup
Preparation time: 10 minutes

Ingredients:
1/4 cup lemon juice
1/2 cup olive oil
7 cloves garlic, peeled and crushed with a dash of salt
5 cubes potatoes, fried until tender
1/2 teaspoon salt

Steps:
1) Mash potatoes finely in a bowl.
2) Process mashed potato with garlic, oil, lemon juice, and salt until smooth and thick.
3) Serve in small bowls next to grills.

Sesame Paste Sauce Taratour

This appetizer is served with fish and meat dishes.

Serves: 3
Preparation time: 15 minutes

Ingredients:
1/2 cup sesame paste
1/4 cup water
1/2 cup lemon juice
3 cloves garlic, crushed with 1/2 teaspoon salt
1/4 cup finely chopped fresh parsley

Steps:
1) Place sesame paste in mixing bowl. Add water, and lemon juice gradually with constant beating (use a fork).
2) When you have a consistent mixture. Add garlic and beat well.
3) Add lemon juice and salt to taste. It should have a sharp taste. Mix with parsley.

Basic Dough

Al ajeena al assasiya

Serves: 8
Preparation time: 25 minutes

Ingredients:

1 kg (32 oz/5 cups) plain flour
1 ¼ cups tepid water
½ cup olive oil
½ cup vegetable oil
2 tablespoons salt
2 tablespoons sugar

Steps:

1) Sift the flour into a working surface.
2) Mix in salt and sugar. Make a well in the centre.
3) Pour olive oil and vegetable oil in the well.
4) Mix the dry ingredients into the liquid.
5) Add water gradually. Knead the dough into a ball (if the dough is too stiff add some water).
6) Knead the dough on a floured working surface until it is smooth and elastic this can be done in an electric mixer fitted with a dough hook, or in a food processor.
7) Form the dough into a ball and put into a lightly floured bowl, covered with a damp cloth. Leave in a warm place until the dough has doubled in size - about 6 hours.

Dairies

Makes: 8 cups of yoghurt or ½ kg (16 oz) strained yoghurt

Ingredients:

8 cups milk
½ cup yoghurt
1 teaspoon salt (as desired)

Yoghurt

Steps:

1) Bring milk to a boil. Place aside until tepid.
2) Stir in yoghurt. Cover pot with lid. Wrap pot with a wool cover. Place in a warm place for 6 hours.
3) Remove lid. Stir in salt. Cool in refrigerator for 3 hours.

Strained Yoghurt

Steps:

1) Pour the cold yoghurt into a cheese cloth bag.
2) Tie and let hang for 12 hours.

Note: You should double the time of straining the yoghurt when you double the quantity of yoghurt.

Cooked Yoghurt

Ingredients:

1 ½ kg (48 oz) plain yoghurt

2 tablespoons cornstarch
1 teaspoon salt
1 cup water
1 beaten egg (or egg's white)

Steps:

1) Strain yoghurt using a smooth colander into a pot. Add egg or egg's white.
2) Dissolve cornstarch in 1 cup of water. Stir into cold yoghurt for 2 minutes.
3) Place on medium heat, stirring constantly until it boils.
4) Remove from heat and use as desired.

Preparing Nuts

Sesame:

Buy toasted or toast without butter or oil.

Pine Nuts:

Remove any impurities. Fry in some oil.

Almonds:

a) Soak almonds in boiling water for 20 minutes.
b) Remove, peel, and flake.
c) Wash then drain well. Fry in some oil.

Peanuts:

Toast in a pan without oil. Remove and place aside until cool. Peel and flake.

Pistachio Nuts:

Soak in boiling water for 20 minutes.

Remove, peel and flake. Wash, drain well, and then fry in some oil.

Walnuts:

Soak in cold water for about 1 hour or until lighter in color. Wash well, drain, and then fry in some oil.

Cashews:

Wash well. Drain then fry in some oil.

Hazelnuts:

Toast in an oven or in a pan without oil. Remove, place aside until cool, peel, and flake.

Oven Temperature

Electrical

	°C	°F
very low	120	250
low	150	300
low to moderate	160-180	325-350
moderate	180-200	375-400
moderate to high	210-230	425-450
high	240-250	475-500
very high	260	525-550

Gas

	°C	°F
very low	120	250
low	150	300
low to moderate	160	325
moderate	180	350
moderate to high	190	375
high	200	400
very high	230	450

Measuring Up

$1/4$ cup = 60ml
$1/3$ cup = 85ml
$1/2$ cup = 125 ml
$2/3$ cup = 170 ml
$3/4$ cup = 180 ml
1 cup = 250 ml
2 cups = 500 ml
3 cups = 750 ml
4 cups = 1 litre
$1/4$ teaspoon = 1.5 ml
$1/2$ teaspoon = 3 ml
$3/4$ teaspoon = 4 ml
1 teaspoon = 5 ml
1 tablespoon = 15 ml

Quick Converter		
g	oz	ml
30	1	30
60	2	60
125	4	125
250	8	250
370	12	370
500	16	500
1 pound = 450 g		

SALADS

The origin of the word salad is the Latin sal or "salt". Its adoption is believed to have grown out of the ancient Roman habit of dipping greens in salt before eating.

Today salad reaches far beyond that narrow definition. Almost any ingredient can be turned into a salad : All vegetables, lettuce and other leaves, and all manner of beans, pulses and grains.

When we talk about good cooking, we invariably single out the use of fresh ingredients. That is one reason why salads are so popular.

That freshness also carries with it the benefit of good health. For it is low in fat and calories, high in dietary fiber, rich with vitamins and minerals.

Salads can be served as casual or elegant appetizer or accompaniments, or as an entire meal in itself.

I hope you will enjoy preparing, in no time, our absolutely simple salad making. You can start with Fatoush, serve Beetroot and Sesame Paste salad to accompany main meals, or serve Tabbouleh that stands out as a star on your table.

The main dressing needed for these salads is a combination of crushed garlic, lemon juice and extra virgin olive oil. Pomegranate thickened juice is a very tasty liquid that can be purchased from any Middle Eastern supermarkets, it adds a special flavor to many salads. Vinegar, pomegranate juice and lemon juice are three important ingredients that can substitute one another.

Enjoy the different tastes offered by our different salads.

Parsley Salad

Tabbouleh

The most famous Lebanese salad, made of: parsley, tomato, mint and burghul.

Serves: 5
Preparation time: 40 minutes

Ingredients:

¼ cup burghul, fine cracked wheat
2 cups finely chopped parsley
*½ kg (16 oz) firm red tomatoes, washed and
    finely chopped*
½ cup finely chopped fresh mint leaves
¼ cup finely chopped onion
½ cup lemon juice
1 teaspoon salt (as desired)
½ cup extra virgin olive oil
a dash of all spice (as desired)

Steps:

1. Wash chopped mint and parsley then drain well.
2. Wash the burghul several times and drain. Soak in chopped tomatoes for 20 minutes.
3. Rub chopped onion with salt. Mix all ingredients in a bowl. Add olive oil and lemon juice, toss the mixture well.
4. Serve Tabbouleh with crisp cos lettuce leaves, or fresh cabbage leaves.

Artichoke and Mushroom Salad

Salatet al ardichawke
maa al fiter

A unique salad for artichoke lovers.

Serves: 4
Preparation time: 10 minutes

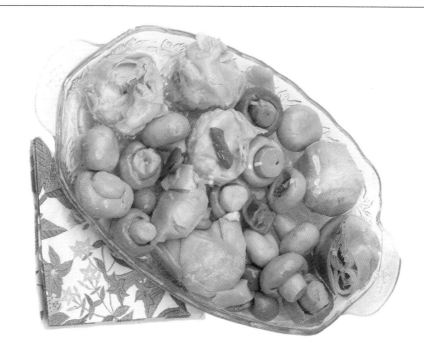

Ingredients:

500 g (16 oz) canned artichoke
500 g (16 oz) canned mushrooms
$^1/_4$ cup chopped parsley
2 cloves garlic, crushed with a dash of salt
$^1/_2$ cup lemon juice
a dash of olive oil

Steps:

1. Wash canned ingredients. Place in a bowl.
2. Mix garlic, lemon juice, olive oil, and parsley in the bowl.
3. Serve accompanied by different dishes.

Purslane and Cucumber Salad

Salatet al bakla maa al khyar

A delicious and nutritious salad. Perfect as a companion for many main plates.

Serves: 3
Preparation time: 10 minutes

Ingredients:

1 cup purslane leaves
2 cucumbers, sliced into rings
¼ cup lemon juice
½ teaspoon salt
¼ cup olive oil

Steps:

1. Mix well all the above ingredients. Place in a serving platter. Serve.

Tunisian Salad

Salata Tunisia

A delicious and nutritious salad with striking colors.

Serves: 5
Preparation time: 20 minutes

Ingredients:

2 red bell peppers, finely chopped
2 green bell peppers, finely chopped
2 cucumbers, finely chopped
1 spring onion, finely chopped
2 medium tomatoes, peeled and finely chopped
a dash of salt
a dash of ground white pepper

½ cup lemon juice
¼ cup olive oil

Steps:

1. Mix well all the above ingredients. Serve immediately.

Beetroot and Sesame Paste Salad

Salatet al shamandar bil-tahini

This salad is usually served with seafood.

Serves: 5

Preparation time: about 20 minutes

Cooking time: 1 hour

Ingredients:

1 kg (32 oz) beetroots, boiled till tender (about 1 hour)

¹/₂ cup sesame paste

¹/₂ cup lemon juice

1 tablespoon finely chopped fresh parsley

1 teaspoon salt (as desired)

Steps:

1. Peel beetroots and cut into cubes.
2. Blend well sesame paste, salt, lemon juice and parsley. Adjust taste by water or lemon juice.
3. Pour over beetroot cubes and mix to coat.
4. Serve it as a side dish with fish.

Note: You can add minced onion to this salad. You can also substitute beetroots with boiled and chopped swiss-chard's stems.

Thyme Salad

Salatet al zaatar alakhdar

A tasty appetizer.

Serves: 2
Preparation time: 15 minutes

Ingredients:

1 bunch thyme
¹/₄ cup lemon juice
¹/₄ teaspoon salt
2 tablespoons olive oil
1 small onion, finely chopped

Steps:

1. Pick thyme leaves, wash well, drain, squeeze with your hands.
2. Rub onion well with salt in a bowl. Mix with lemon juice and olive oil. Add to thyme and toss well.
3. Serve accompanied by different grills.

Note: Adding 1 tablespoon of pomegranate thickened juice to this salad would give a special taste.

Lima Beans Salad

Salatet al fasoulya al bayda

This appetizer is usually served with main dishes.

Serves: 5
Preparation time: about 1 hour
Cooking time: 45 minutes

Ingredients:

2 cups Lima beans (soaked for 1 night)
2 cloves garlic, crushed with a dash of salt
¹/₄ cup lemon juice
¹/₂ cup finely chopped fresh parsley
¹/₂ cup extra virgin olive oil
¹/₂ teaspoon salt

Steps:

1. Wash beans and drain. Add water to cover. Bring to a boil over medium heat. Reduce heat to low. Cover and simmer for 45 minutes or till tender.
2. Dressing: Mix well salt, garlic, lemon juice, oil and parsley.
3. Drain beans and pour dressing over.
4. Serve hot or cold.

Cucumber and Yoghurt Salad

Salatet al laban bil khyar

A tasty refreshing salad, best served with rice dishes.

Serves: 6

Preparation time: about 20 minutes

Ingredients:

500 (16 oz) cucumbers, diced
3 cups yoghurt
3 cloves garlic, crushed with a dash of salt
1 teaspoon salt (as desired)
1 teaspoon dried ground mint
1 cup water

Steps:

1. Blend well yoghurt and water till consistent.
2. Add cucumber, garlic, salt and mint. Blend well.
3. Serve cold.

Broad Beans and Artichoke Salad

Salatet al Foul wal Ardi Chawki

A delicious and easy to prepare salad.

Serves: 4
Preparation time: 10 minutes

Ingredients:

500 g (16 oz) artichoke (canned)
1 cup green broad beans, peeled
¹/₄ cup lemon juice
¹/₄ cup olive oil
2 cloves garlic, crushed with a dash of salt

Steps:

1. Wash aritchoke. Halve.
2. Place broad beans in centre of a serving bowl. Arrange the artichoke halves around it.
3. Mix well garlic, lemon juice, and olive oil. Sprinkle lemon juice mixture over the broad beans and artichoke.

Cabbage and Tomato Salad

Salatet al malfouf wal tamatem

Raw cabbage, either green or white, makes an excellent salad.

Serves: 5

Preparation time: about 30 minutes

Ingredients:

¹/₂ medium sized cabbage
2 medium tomatoes, washed and sliced
¹/₄ cup lemon juice or 3 tablespoons vinegar
2 cloves garlic, crushed with a dash of salt
1 teaspoon salt (as desired)
¹/₄ cup extra virgin olive oil

Steps:

1. Remove and discard the larger leaves from the cabbage, then cut it lengthwise into quarters. Cut each quarter into long, very thin strips. Wash and drain.
2. Mix well garlic with salt, lemon juice and oil.
3. In a salad bowl, mix the cabbage strips with garlic mixture.
4. Garnish with tomato slices and serve.

Mixed Green Salad

Salatet al khoudar
al moonawa

A nutritious salad.

Serves: 4
**Preparation time: 30
minutes**

Ingredients:

¹/₂ kg (16 oz) red tomatoes, cubed
¹/₂ kg (16 oz) cucumbers, cut into rounds
¹/₂ medium Cos lettuce, broken into small pieces
1 green sweet pepper, coarsely chopped
1 medium sized onion, coarsely chopped
¹/₂ bunch purslane leaves, washed
¹/₂ cup fresh mint leaves, washed
3 cloves garlic crushed with a dash of salt
¹/₄ cup olive oil
¹/₄ cup lemon juice
*1 tablespoon pomegranate thickened juice
  (optional)*
1 teaspoon salt (as desired)

Steps:

1. Put all vegetables in a bowl. Mix garlic, olive
   oil, lemon juice, salt and pomegranate juice.
   Add to vegetables, toss well.
2. Serve immediately accompanied by different
   dishes.

Toasted Bread Salad

Al Fattoush

A delicious Lebanese salad containing toasted bread, parsley, tomato and other vegetables.

Serves: 5
Preparation time: 30 minutes

Ingredients:

$^1/_2$ *Lebanese round bread (pitta), toasted*
3 medium firm tomatoes, washed and chopped
3 slender cucumbers (250g/19 oz), washed and chopped
3 medium radishes (250g/19 oz) (1 cup), washed and chopped
4 spring onions, washed and coarsely chopped
1 medium onion ($^1/_4$ cup), roughly chopped
$^1/_2$ *cup lemon juice*
2 cloves garlic, crushed with a pinch of salt
$^1/_2$ *teaspoon dried mint*
2 tablespoons vinegar
$^1/_2$ *cup olive oil*
1 cup coarsely chopped fresh mint leaves
1 cup coarsely chopped parsley
1 cup small purslane leaves
$^1/_2$ *teaspoon ground sumac*
$^1/_2$ *cup coarsely chopped sweet green pepper*
1 teaspoon salt
8 crisp cos (2 cups) lettuce leaves, torn into bite size pieces
$^1/_2$ *Lebanease round pitta bread, toasted (extra)*

Steps:

1. Break toasted bread into small pieces and keep aside.
2. Wash the chopped mint, parsley and purslane, then drain well.
3. Mix crushed garlic with salt, oil, vinegar, dried mint, lemon juice and ground sumac and keep aside.
4. Put all ingredients in a serving bowl. Add toasted bread pieces and dress with garlic mixture, mix well.
5. Serve fattoush if you wish garnished with additional toasted bread.

APPETIZERS

The Lebanese Kitchen is known for its excellent selection of appetizers. A very big variety of recipes from there and from other countries, rich and tasty, has been chosen to suit your taste.

You can prepare and serve them with ease as the featured attraction of a cocktail party or informal buffet -that is as Meza, or you can present them as the first course of a meal - that is, as appetizers. And also you can indeed make up an entire light main meal based on them alone.

Every one of the dishes in this section has been created not only to be delicious, but also to be exceptionally easy to prepare. With that in mind, let me offer one final word of encouragement: Try a selection of these recipes as soon as possible, perhaps even for dinner tonight.

I'm sure you will agree that well chosen Meza and appetizers are capable of making any party or meal feel like a special occasion.

Fried Omelet Balls

Akras al iggi al maklia

Delicious omelet balls of eggs and vegetables.

Serves: 4

Preparation time: 30 minutes

Frying time: 30 minutes

Ingredients:

¹/₂ cup fresh parsley, washed and finely chopped
6 eggs
¹/₂ cup finely chopped onion
¹/₄ cup plain flour
2 medium zucchini, finely chopped
1 sweet pepper, washed and grated
¹/₂ teaspoon salt (as desired)
¹/₄ teaspoon ground allspice (as desired)
¹/₄ teaspoon ground chili pepper
¹/₄ teaspoon baking powder
lemon zest
2 cups vegetable oil

Steps:

1. Wash chopped parsley and drain well. Mix chopped onions, salt, spices, parsley, chopped sweet pepper, and zucchini.
2. In another bowl, mix flour with baking powder then add to vegetable mixture. Blend eggs in a separate bowl, stir-in lemon zest. Add the mixture to vegetable mixture and stir.
3. Heat oil in a pan, pour in a spoonful of omelet.
4. Turn over each ball till it is golden-brown from both sides (repeat the process with the remaining mixture).
5. Serve balls warm with salad and fried potatoes.

Note: you can substitute whole zucchini with its cores.

Eggplant with Sesame Paste

Motabal al bathinjan

A sensational appetizer that is served with most meals.

Serves: 5
Preparation time: 30 minutes
Cooking time: 15 minutes

Ingredients:

2 large eggplants, about 1 kg (32 oz)
¹/₄ cup lemon juice (as desired)
¹/₄ cup sesame seed paste
3 cloves garlic crushed with ¹/₂ tablespoon salt (as desired)
1 teaspoon white vinegar
2 tablespoons parsley, finely chopped

Steps:

1. Grill eggplants on high heat for 15 minutes after piercing them by a fork on all sides. Turning frequently.
2. When tender, wash under running water then peel off skin while hot and remove stem. Pound to a purée (use a food processor, if available). Blend in gradually sesame paste, lemon juice, and vinegar. When mixture is consistent, add garlic and beat mixture well. If thick, adjust by lemon juice and water.
3. Serve it garnished with parsley, red pepper and olive oil.

Eggplant Casserole

Msakaet al bathinjan (al magmour)

An exotic appetizer. Try it.

Serves: 5
Preparation time: 30 minutes
Cooking time: 30 minutes

Ingredients:

1 kg (32 oz) eggplants, peeled and thickly cut,
* lengthwise*
1 kg (32 oz) tomatoes, peeled and sliced
1 cup of dried chickpeas, cooked (see p.9) or
* canned, washed and drained*
1 cup of quartered and sliced onion
2 tablespoons ground dried mint
10 cloves garlic, fried in oil
6 cloves garlic, crushed with a dash of salt
2 cups vegetable oil (or to cover eggplants)
1 teaspoon salt (as desired)
a dash of sugar
1 fresh red or green chili

Steps:

1. Sprinkle salt over eggplant slices. Fry eggplants till golden brown and drain on paper towels.
2. Fry onion rings until soft. Stir in garlic until golden.
3. Add tomatoes, chickpeas, chili, salt and sugar. Bring to a boil for 5 minutes.
4. Add fried eggplants. Cover pot, cook on moderate heat for 10 minutes.
5. Mix dry mint with crushed garlic. Add mint mixture to pot. Cook for 2 minutes.
6. Remove chili and serve cold with main dishes.

Okra in Oil

Bamyi bi-zayt

A delicious appetizer.

Serves: 5
Preparation time: 15 minutes
Cooking time: 30 minutes

Ingredients:

700 g (1 ¹/₂ lb) fresh okra / frozen or canned, trim stem end and wash
1 kg (32 oz) tomatoes, washed and sliced
1 cup finely chopped onion
2 heads garlic, peeled
1 teaspoon salt (as desired)
¹/₂ cup vegetable oil or olive oil
1 cup finely chopped fresh coriander, washed
1 tablespoon ground dried coriander
4 cloves garlic, crushed
1 fresh red or green chili
1 cup water
a dash of ground allspice
a dash of sugar

Steps:

1. Fry okra in oil. Remove and put on paper towels.
2. Fry onions in oil till transparent. Add dried coriander and garlic. Stir for 2 minutes till fragrant.
3. Add tomatoes. Cook over medium heat for another 2 minutes.
4. Add okra, salt, sugar, allspice, chili, and water. Bring to a boil over medium heat and cook for 25 minutes or till okra is tender. Add fresh coriander and boil for 2 minutes.
5. Remove chili and serve cold.

Potato with Coriander

Batata harra

A delicious appetizer of fried potatoes with fresh coriander.

Serves: 4

Preparation time: 15 minutes

Cooking time: 30 minutes

Ingredients:

1 kg (32 oz) potatoes
2 cups vegetable oil (for frying)
4 cloves garlic, crushed with a pinch of salt
1 teaspoon salt (as desired)
¹/₂ teaspoon ground red pepper (as desired)
2 tablespoons finely chopped fresh coriander
a dash of dried coriander

Steps:

1. Wash the fresh coriander, drain and put on a clean piece of cloth to dry (5 minutes). Peel the potatoes, wash and cut into small cubes, rewash and drain.
2. Fry the potatoes in hot oil until golden-brown, put on absorbent paper.
3. Mix the garlic with salt and fry in hot oil for 5 minutes till fragrant. Add to it the potatoes, a dash of dry coriander, and the red pepper.
4. Stir well for 2 minutes. Stir in fresh coriander then remove from heat.
5. Serve hot.

Chickpeas Purée

Hummus bil tahini

It is the number one appetizer in Lebanon.

Serves: 4
Preparation time: 30 minutes

Ingredients:

1 cup cooked chickpeas (see p. 9) or canned
$^1/_2$ teaspoon salt
2 cloves garlic, crushed with a pinch of salt
$^1/_4$ cup lemon juice
2 tablespoons sesame paste
2 tablespoons parsley, finely chopped
$^1/_2$ teaspoon ground cumin

Steps:

1. Drain warm chickpeas and reserve 1 tablespoon. Beat chickpeas in a food processor.
2. Blend chickpeas with the sesame paste, lemon juice, crushed garlic, and salt into a purée. Adjust flavor and consistency with lemon juice and salt if necessary (Hummus should be thick and smooth).
3. Serve in Hummus bowls. Pour olive oil in center and garnish with the reserved chickpeas, chopped parsley and cumin.

Chickpeas in Oil

Humus bil zayt (hummus balila)

Usually this Lebanese dish is prepared for breakfast when all the family members are around.

Serves: 3
Preparation time: 20 minutes
Soaking time: 12 hours (see p. 9)

Ingredients:

*1 cup cooked chickpeas (see p.9) / or canned
  chickpeas
2 tablespoons lemon juice
1/4 cup olive oil
4 tablespoons butter
1 teaspoon ground cumin (as desired)
1 teaspoon ground cinnamon (as desired)
1/2 cup pine nuts, fried
2 cloves garlic, crushed with a dash of salt*

Steps:

1. Drain warm chickpeas. Put in a bowl. Mix with garlic, lemon juice, 1/2 teaspoon of cumin, cinnamon and melted butter.
2. Garnish with pine nuts and 1/2 teaspoon of cumin and olive oil.
3. Serve with tomatoes and green onions.

Mallow Leaves in Oil

Khobaizeh bil zayt

A meatless cold dish, good for vegetarians.

Serves: 5
Preparation time: 40 minutes
Cooking time: about 30 minutes

Ingredients:

1 kg (32 oz) green mallow leaves, finely chopped
3 medium onions, peeled and finely chopped
$^1/_2$ cup olive oil
$^1/_2$ cup finely chopped fresh coriander
6 cloves garlic, crushed with a dash of salt
$^1/_2$ teaspoon salt
a dash of black pepper
$^1/_4$ cup water

Steps:

1. Wash mallow leaves several times in a bowl, under running water. Drain, then squeeze with your hands excess water.
2. Fry onions until golden in hot oil. Save some onions for garnishing, add mallow leaves to onion pan. Stir over medium heat. Add garlic, coriander, salt, and pepper.
3. Mix mixture well. Add water. Cover and leave on low heat for 20 minutes or until cooked.
4. Serve cold, garnished with fried onions. Sprinkle over some lemon juice.

Grilled Eggplants with Bell Pepper

Al rahib (baba ganooj)

A delicious appetizer for all times.

Serves: 5
Preparation time: 30 minutes

Ingredients:

1 kg (32 oz) grilled eggplants, washed then peeled
1 green bell pepper, finely chopped
1 medium onion, finely chopped
3 cloves of garlic, crushed with a dash of salt
1/2 kg (16 oz) tomatoes, peeled and finely chopped
1/2 cup lemon juice
1 teaspoon salt
a dash of olive oil

Steps:

1. Process eggplants until smooth
2. Stir in all the above ingredients.
3. Serve in a platter garnished with olive oil and green bell pepper slices.

Bell Pepper with Tomatoes
Shakshouke

An appetizer served usually with fish and meat.

Serves: 4
Preparation time: 30 minutes
Cooking time: 20 minutes

Ingredients:

¹/₂ kg (16 oz) sweet green bell peppers, diced
1 teaspoon dried coriander
¹/₄ cup finely chopped fresh coriander
1 kg (32 oz) tomatoes, peeled and chopped
1 small onion, finely chopped
5 cloves garlic crushed with 1 teaspoon salt (as desired)
¹/₄ teaspoon ground piquant red pepper
¹/₄ cup olive or vegetable oil

Steps:

1. Fry bell peppers in oil for 10 minutes.
2. Stir in onion, garlic, dry and fresh coriander over medium heat. Add tomatoes, ground pepper and simmer till bell pepper is tender.
3. Serve cold.

Lentil with Oil and Lemon Juice

Adas motabal bil zayt wal hamod

A delicious and easy to prepare appetizer.

Serves: 4
Preparation time: 10 minutes
Cooking time: 20 minutes

Steps:

1. Boil lentils on medium heat for 20 minutes or until tender.
2. Stir in garlic, salt, and lemon juice.
3. Serve in a platter. Sprinkle some olive oil over.
4. Serve accompanied by spring onions.

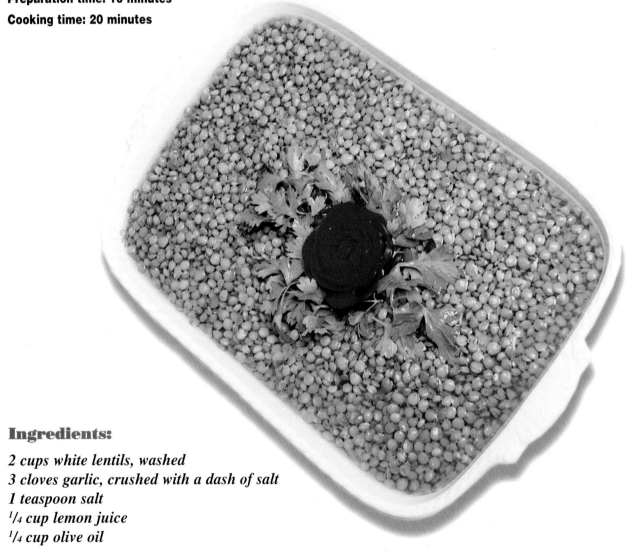

Ingredients:

2 cups white lentils, washed
3 cloves garlic, crushed with a dash of salt
1 teaspoon salt
¹/₄ cup lemon juice
¹/₄ cup olive oil

Grilled Kafta

Arayes

A Lebanese specialty. You can serve it as an appetizer or as a light meal. Delicious and easy to prepare.

Serves: 3
Preparation time: 25 minutes
Cooking time: 5 minutes

Ingredients:

¹/₂ kg (16 oz) kafta (see p.176, step 1)
1 ¹/₂ pitta bread, cut into 12 pieces
2 tablespoons butter

1. Spread some butter on the inner part of bread pieces.
2. Divide kafta into 12 portions. Spread over buttered bread.
3. Put the pieces in a grill or an oven at 200°C/400°F for 5 minutes or till kafta is cooked.
4. Serve hot with yoghurt.

Chili Sauce

Al-mohamara

An exotic Syrian appetizer.

Serves: 5

Preparation / Cooking time: 30 minutes

Ingredients:

12 dried chilies
2 tablespoons ground breadcrumbs
3 medium onions, chopped
1 ¹/₂ cup cleaned walnuts
1 teaspoon salt
1 teaspoon ground cumin
¹/₂ teaspoon ground dried coriander
1 cup olive oil
¹/₂ cup lemon juice
¹/₄ cup pomegranate thickened juice
a dash of ground coffee

Steps:

1. Soak chilies in hot oil until soft. Remove seeds and membranes. Process chilies with onion until the mixture becomes smooth.
2. Add walnuts. Process until smooth.
3. Stir in breadcrumbs, dried coriander, coffee, salt, and cumin.
4. Stir in lemon juice, pomegranate juice, and olive oil.
5. Serve in a platter, garnished with walnuts and olive oil.

Chick Peas in Yoghurt

Fattet al hummus

It is a very tasty and popular dish. You can serve it as an appetizer or as a breakfast.

Serves: 5
Preparation time: 30 minutes

Ingredients:

¹/₂ kg (16 oz) (2 cups) canned chickpeas
5 cups yoghurt
5 cloves garlic, crushed with a dash of salt
2 tablespoons sesame paste
1 teaspoon salt (as desired)
1 toasted pita bread (30 cm in diameter)
3 tablespoons fried pine nuts
¹/₂ teaspoon ground cumin
¹/₂ teaspoon ground red pepper (as desired)
¹/₄ cup melted butter for garnishing
1 teaspoon vinegar
¹/₂ medium size pomegranate
8 cups water
¹/₂ teaspoon bicarbonate of soda

Steps:

1. Blend well yoghurt, garlic, salt, vinegar and sesame paste.
2. Cut pita bread into small pieces. Place in a deep dish.
3. Put hot chickpeas with its liquid (about 2 cups) over the bread. Add yoghurt mixture.
4. Garnish with pine nuts, butter, pomegranate, pepper, and cumin. Serve hot.

Stuffed Eggplant with Yoghurt

Fattet al bathinjan

A famous Syrian dish. It consists of stuffed eggplants with yoghurt.

Serves: 5
Preparation time: 40 minutes
Cooking time: 50 minutes

Ingredients:

1 kg (32 oz) small eggplants
400 g (14 oz) minced meat
¹/₂ cup fried pine nuts
1 cup tomato juice or paste
2 tablespoons pomegranate thickened juice
1 cup water
1 teaspoon salt (as desired)
a dash of ground black pepper
a dash of ground cinnamon
4 cups yoghurt
6 cloves garlic crushed with a dash of salt
2 toasted pitta bread
2 cups vegetable oil (for frying the eggplants)
2 tablespoons butter (for frying minced meat)
2 tablespoons melted butter for garnishing

Steps:

1. Fry minced meat in butter then add peppers and salt. Mix well on low heat for 10 minutes. Put aside.
2. Roll eggplant on a surface, so that hollowing would be easier.
3. Wash eggplants well. Remove stem ends.
4. Hollow out with an apple corer. Wash well again. Drain.
5. Mix fried meat and half the quantity of pine nuts. Fill the eggplants with meat mixture. Fry the stuffed eggplants in oil then put aside.
6. Put tomato juice in a pan then add water, pomegranate and salt. Stir to mix.
7. Add the stuffed eggplants to the tomato mixture. Bring to a boil. Lower heat and leave for 40 minutes or until tender and ¹/₂ cup of the liquid is left.
8. Cut toasted pita bread into small pieces. Put in a heavy based plate. Add eggplants and liquid. Mix yoghurt with garlic then add them to the plate.
9. Sprinkle the fried pine nuts and butter over the yoghurt. Serve hot.

Note: You can garnish this dish also with minced meat.

Broad Bean Patties

Falafel

The Egyptian and Lebanese kitchens are known for the delicious FALAFEL made mainly from beans.

Serves: 6

Preparation time: 1 hour 30 minutes

Cooking time: 30 minutes

Ingredients:

1 kg (32 oz) peeled green fava beans (dried)
1 cup roughly chopped fresh parsley
1 cup roughly chopped fresh coriander
3 heads garlic, peeled and crushed
3 large onions, chopped
$^1/_2$ teaspoon ground cinnamon
$^1/_2$ teaspoon ground cumin
2 teaspoons salt
1 teaspoon ground paprika
1 teaspoon ground chili
$^1/_2$ teaspoon ground black pepper
2 tablespoons plain flour
1 teaspoon ground dried coriander
$^1/_2$ teaspoon bicarbonate of soda
3 teaspoons baking powder
5 cups vegetable oil (for deep frying)

Steps:

1. Soak the beans in water for 24 hours, then drain well.
2. Mix all ingredients except (salt, cumin, cinnamon, paprika, black pepper, chili, bicarbonate, and baking powder).
3. Grind in a food processor.
4. Add to the mixture salt, peppers, bicarbonate, baking powder and process another time.
5. Leave mixture aside for 30 minutes then knead.
6. Divide mixture into balls using a special tool for Falafel balls, if this tool is not available take a spoonful of mixture and make flat balls. Heat oil in deep pan over high heat, then fry till browned.
7. Serve Falafel hot with parsley, tomatoes, fresh mint, spring onions, pickles and sesame paste.

Dried Fava Beans in Oil

Fool medammes

The most popular Arabian breakfast, almost every region has more than a restaurant specialized in serving this dish.

Serves: 3
Preparation time: 30 minutes
Soaking time: 24 hours

Ingredients:

1 cup cooked fava beans (see p.9) / or canned fava beans
1/2 cup lemon juice
3 cloves garlic crushed with 1 teaspoon salt (as desired)
2 tablespoons finely chopped fresh parsley
1/2 cup olive oil

Steps:

1. Drain the warm fava beans. Put in a bowl. Mix garlic, lemon juice and 1/2 quantity of oil. Add to beans and mix well.
2. Garnish with parsley and olive oil.
3. Serve with spring onions and tomatoes.

Stuffed Eggplants in Oil

Bathinjan bi-zayt

The best of stuffed vegetables.

Serves: 5
Preparation time: 1 hour
Cooking time: 1 hour

Ingredients:

1 kg (32 oz) small and long eggplants
$^1/_4$ cup finely chopped fresh mint leaves
$^1/_2$ cup finely chopped onion
1 kg (32 oz) finely chopped tomatoes
2 cups finely chopped parsley
1 cup olive oil and vegetable oil mixture
$^1/_2$ cup short grain rice
1 teaspoon salt (as desired)
$^1/_2$ cup lemon juice
a dash of ground white pepper
2 medium potatoes cut into slices
1 teaspoon pomegranate thickened juice (optional)
1 $^1/_2$ cups water or to cover 3 cm above the stuffed eggplants
a dash of ground allspice
a dash of ground cinnamon

Steps:

1. Prepare filling as the Warak Enab Bi-Zayt (see p. step 1).
2. Roll each eggplant between your hands to make hollowing out the eggplants easier.
3. Cut off eggplants stem ends, using a sharp knife.
4. Hollow using an apple corer or a special zucchini corer, removing the pulp and leaving a $^3/_4$ cm thick wall (be careful not to pierce walls).
5. Fill the eggplants with filling. Don't over stuff. Reserve filling's stock. Pour $^1/_2$ cup of oil and arrange potato slices at the bottom of a pot. Lay side by side stuffed eggplants over the potato slices. Invert a plate on top of the eggplants.
6. Add lemon juice, filling's stock, pomegranate juice, water, and oil. Bring to a boil on high heat. Cover, reduce heat and simmer for one hour or until tender.
7. Serve cold garnished with potato slices.

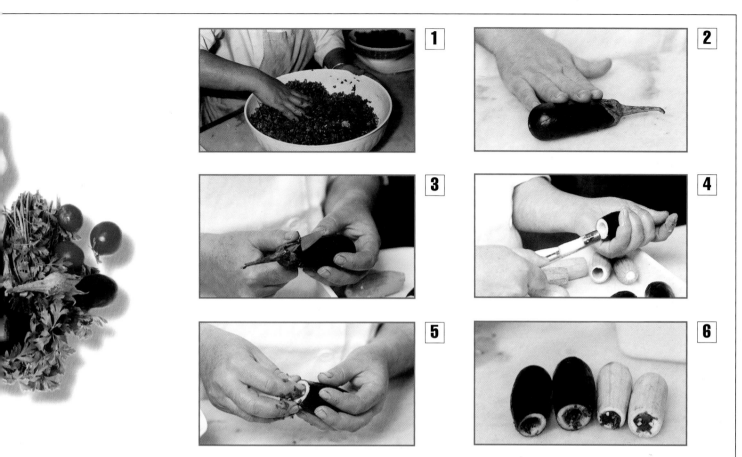

Stuffed Zucchini in Oil

Kousa Mahshou bi-zayt

Follow stuffed eggplant in oil recipe (see p. 46).

Raw Kibbi

Kibbi nayye

Kibbi is the main dish in the Levant. Whatever meat you use, trim of all fat and gristle before preparation.

Serves: 6

Preparation time: 30 minutes

Ingredients:

500 g (16 oz) ground lean beef or lamb
1 cup fine burghul
1 small onion, peeled
$^1/_2$ teaspoon ground allspice
$^1/_2$ teaspoon ground cinnamon
1 teaspoon salt (as desired)
1 tablespoon pine nuts and few fresh mint leaves
   for garnish
8 fresh basil leaves
8 fresh marjoram leaves
$^1/_4$ cup cleaned walnuts
Virgin olive oil

Steps:

1. Rinse burghul, drain in a sieve and press with back of spoon to remove as much moisture as possible. Strain again with your hands to make sure it is dry.
2. Process with onion, marjoram and basil.
3. Mix meat with burghul, salt, allspice and cinnamon. Dip your hands in cold water and knead the mixture. Keep your hands wet. Knead till mixture is firm and smooth.
4. Place on platter and shape into a flat round. Dip hands into cold water and smooth all over.
5. Serve garnished with pine nuts, walnuts, mint leaves and some virgin olive oil.

Note: If you desire piquant raw kibbi, add red dried hot chilies to burghul when processing it with onion, majoram, and basil.

Dandelion Leaves in Oil

Hindbeh bi-zayt

Perfect for hot summer lunches.

Serves: 5
Preparation time: 30 minutes
Cooking time: 30 minutes

Ingredients:

1 kg (32 oz) dandelion
1/2 cup olive oil
1 cup finely chopped parsley
5 onions (1/2 kg/16 oz) sliced into thin rings
3 garlic cloves crushed with a sprinkle of salt
1/2 tablespoon salt (as desired)
a dash of bicarbonate of soda

Steps:

1. Remove yellow leaves from dandelion. Wash well. Finely chop.
2. Bring water to a boil then add bicarbonate of soda and dandelion and cook over medium heat for 5 minutes.
3. Drain and rinse in cold water, then squeeze until dry.
4. Fry onion until golden. Remove 1/2 quantity of onions from oil, reserve aside. Fry chopped leaves in the same oil with onions for 15 minutes. Add garlic, coriander and salt and fry for 5 minutes.
5. Place in a serving plate and garnish with the reserved onions. Serve cold with some lemon juice.

Green Beans in Oil

Lubya bi-zayt

Perfect for hot summer lunches.

Serves: 5
Preparation time: 15 minutes
Cooking time: 1 hour

Ingredients:

*1 kg (32 oz) green beans, string and snip off the
ends, snip each bean into two and wash
1 kg (32 oz) tomatoes, washed, peeled and
chopped
1 ¹/₂ cups finely chopped onion
¹/₂ cup olive oil or vegetable oil
¹/₂ teaspoon salt (as desired)
a dash of ground allspice
a dash of sugar
3 heads garlic, peeled
1 fresh green or red chili
¹/₂ cup water*

Steps:

1. Fry onion and garlic cloves in oil over high
   heat, stir for 5 minutes.
2. Add beans, cook for 10 minutes, stir
   occasionally.
3. Add tomato, salt, sugar, chili, allspice, and
   water. Cover. Bring to a boil.
4. Cook over low heat for 35 minutes or till tender.
5. Remove chili then serve cold with spring

Fried Liver
Kibed makli

A nutritious appetizer served before a main meal or as a brunch.

Serves: 5
Preparation time: 15 minutes
Cooking time: 20 minutes

Ingredients:

$1/2$ kg (16 oz) chicken liver, small cubes (remove thin transparent layer)
3 large onions, sliced
$1/2$ teaspoon salt (as desired)
$1/2$ teaspoon ground hot black pepper (as desired)
$1/2$ teaspoon ground allspice
$1/2$ cup lemon juice or 2 tablespoons pomegranate juice or 1 tablespoon balsamic vinegar
2 tablespoons butter

Steps:

1. Fry onion with butter on medium heat until golden.
2. Add liver cubes, salt and spices. Stir occasionally, for 10 minutes or until tender.
3. Pour lemon juice or pomegranate, mix gently and cook for 2 minutes.
4. Serve hot with lemon wedges.

Stuffed Swiss-Chard Leaves in Oil

Solk bi -zayt

Best when refrigerated before serving.

Serves: 4

Preparation time: $^{1}/_{2}$ hour

Cooking time: 1 hour

Ingredients:

1 kg (32 oz) Swiss-chard
4 cups (4 bunches) finely chopped fresh parsley
$^{1}/_{4}$ cup mint leaves, finely chopped
$^{3}/_{4}$ cup short grain rice
1 large onion, finely chopped
1 kg (32 oz) tomatoes, finely chopped
1 cup olive oil and vegetable oil mixture

$^{1}/_{2}$ tablespoon salt
a dash of ground white pepper
a dash of ground cinnamon
a dash of ground allspice
$^{1}/_{2}$ cup lemon juice
1 teaspoon pomegranate thickened juice (as desired)
1 cup water

Steps:

1. Prepare filling as the Warak Enab Bi-Zayt (see p. 54 -step 1).
2. Silverbeet or Swiss-chard leaves should be halved lengthwise and cut into 15 cm squares.
3. Dip briefly in boiling water. Drain.
4. Place squares shiny side down on work surface.
5. Put 1 tablespoon stuffing on each square.
6. Roll up into a small neat roll.
7. Repeat the same process with the remaining

leaves. Reserve filling's stock.

8. Arrange rolls in layers in an oiled pot. Add water, lemon juice, pomegranate juice, filling's stock, and remaining oil. Invert a plate on top of the rolls to keep them intact during cooking.
9. Place pot over heat. Bring to a boil on medium heat, reduce to low and simmer gently for 45 minutes.
10. Serve luke warm or cold.

Stuffed Grape Vine Leaves in Oil

Warak Enab Bi-Zayt

It is considered the best appetizer by everybody.

Serves: 5
Preparation time: 1 hour
Cooking time: 1 hour

Ingredients:

500 g (16 oz) grape vine leaves
4 cups (4 bunches) finely chopped fresh parsley
1/4 cup finely chopped fresh mint
1/2 cup short grain rice
1 kg (32 oz) finely chopped tomatoes
1 teaspoon salt
 a dash of allspice
1 cup olive oil and vegetable oil mixture
2 medium onions, finely chopped
3 cups water
2 medium potatoes, peeled and sliced into rounds
3/4 cup lemon juice
1 teaspoon pomegranate thickened juice (optional)
a dash of ground cinnamon
a dash of ground white pepper

Steps:

1. Filling: Rub onions with salt. Mix rice with onion, mint, tomato and parsley. Stir in 1/2 quantity of lemon juice, 1/2 quantity of olive oil, salt, and spices.
2. Snip off vine leaves stems if necessary. Rinse in cold water and blanch in boiling water for 2 minutes in 3 or 4 lots. Remove with slotted spoon and place in cold water.
3. Place a vine leaf shiny side down on work surface.
4. Place about a tablespoon of stuffing near stem end.
5. Fold end and sides over stuffing and roll up firmly. Repeat the same process with the remaining leaves.
6. Place 1/2 cup oil in a heavy pan line base of the heavy pan with potato rounds and pack vine leaves rolls close together in layers.
7. Invert a heavy plate on top to keep rolls in shape during cooking.
8. Add 1/2 cup lemon juice , pomegranate juice, filling's stock and 3 cups water. Cover, bring to a boil over moderate heat. Reduce the heat and let simmer for one hour or until tender.
9. Serve cold, garnished with potato slices.

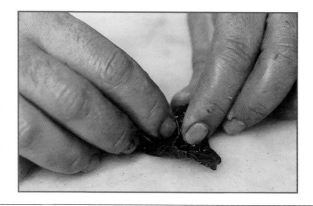

55

Seasoned Brains

Nikhaat bil hamod wal-zayt

A very nutritious appetizer.

Serves: 3
Preparation time: 15 minutes
Cooking time: 20 minutes

Ingredients:

3 sheep's brain
1 large onion, peeled and halved
1 lemon wedge
1 cinnamon stick
a dash of salt
3 cloves garlic, crushed with a dash of salt
$^1\!/_2$ cup lemon juice
olive oil
3 bay leaves

Steps:

1. Remove the thin membrane of the brain under running water. Place in a pot. Cover with water. Add a dash of salt, cinnamon sticks, onion, and lemon wedge.
2. Bring to a boil over moderate heat. Skim off scum and remove lemon wedge. Leave on heat for 10 minutes.
3. Drain the brains. Wash under running cold water. Drain well and place in plate.
4. Add salt, garlic, lemon juice, and a dash of olive oil.
5. Serve garnished with radishes.

PASTRIES

Nobody can say that he does not like pastries. Especially Arabs, who love preparing them almost daily although they take a lot of time and patience to prepare. A large variety of pastries exist in the Arab world cuisine. You can use frozen or ready pastries for speed and convenience.

Filo pastries, are extensively used. These are delicious fried or baked, filled with cheese, meat, chicken and vegetables. The basic dough is also very commonly used, to prepare spinach pies, meat pastries, and sambusik.

Savoury pies will keep well refrigerated for several days. They may be warmed up for serving. The flavor and texture will return to freshly baked.

In this section, we offer you pastries that can be served as a breakfast, snack, appetizer, or as a light meal. We suggest and encourage you to try our thyme manakish pastries during breakfast accompanied with tea.

Green Pea Pastries

Oozi

One of the most popular and tasty pastries in Syria. It consists of rice, meat, and green peas.

Serves: 7
Preparation time: 30 minutes
cooking time: 1 hour

Ingredients:

2 cups rice
1 cup green peas
$\frac{1}{2}$ kg (16 oz) minced meat
2 tablespoons fried pine nuts
2 tablespoons blanched, fried almonds
500 g (16 oz) puff pastry
4 tablespoons shortening or butter
a dash of salt and pepper (as desired)
4 $\frac{1}{2}$ cups water
$\frac{1}{4}$ cup shortening or butter
1 egg, beaten with a dash of white pepper

Steps:

1. Fry minced meat in shortening with a dash of salt and pepper. Cook until tender. Drain and put aside.
2. Wash rice and soak for $\frac{1}{4}$ hour in lukewarm water. Fry peas for 5 minutes in the same shortening. Add $4\frac{1}{2}$ cups of water, bring to a boil for 15 minutes. Add rice, salt, and pepper. Cover and cook for 25 minutes on low heat. Stir into cooked rice and peas: minced meat, almonds, and pine nuts.
3. Roll out puff pastry using a rolling pin.
4. Divide into equal squares.
5. Roll out each square so that it would fit in a small bowl.
6. Put 2 tablespoonfuls of rice mixture in the center of each square in the small bowl.
7. Brush sides of pastry with beaten egg.
8. Fold the sides over the rice mixture.
9. Press well in order to have a little bundle shape.
10. Arrange pastries in a greased oven tray. Brush pastries with beaten egg. Garnish with some pine nuts. Place tray in hot oven (200°C/400°F) till golden and cooked.

Moroccan Chicken Pie

Bastila bil dajaj

One of the best Moroccan main meal.

Serves: 4
Preparation time: 1 hour
Cooking time: 1 hour 15 minutes

Ingredients:

16 sheets filo pastry
1 kg (32 oz) medium sized chicken, cut into 8
  pieces
4 hard boiled eggs, halved
$^1/_4$ cup oil
1 kg (32 oz) onion, sliced into rings
$^1/_4$ teaspoon ground ginger
$^1/_2$ teaspoon salt
3 cinnamon sticks
1 cup finely chopped fresh parsley
$^1/_4$ cup icing sugar
1 tablespoon ground cinnamon (for garnishing)
2 tablespoons butter

Steps:

1. Fry the chicken in oil with onion, cinnamon, salt and ginger. Add boiling water to cover ingredients. Cook over medium heat for 45 minutes till chicken is tender. Remove bones from it. Put chicken meat aside.
2. Add parsley to stock. Simmer over low heat till it thickens.
3. Brush a baking dish with butter and place 8 sheets of filo pastry in the dish. Brush filo with butter. Spread chicken, onion, parsley sauce, and the halved eggs over filo in dish. Place the other 8 sheets on top. Brush with butter.
4. Bake on middle shelf in a moderate heat oven (180°C/350°F) till golden brown. Garnish with icing sugar and cinnamon.
5. Serve hot.

Cheese Cigars

Rakaek bil jiben

Loved by children and adults at all times.

Serves: 4

Preparation time: 35 minutes

Cooking time: about 15 minutes

Ingredients:

8 sheets filo pastry
350 g (12 oz) white cheese, (al- ikawi al tishiki)
  grated
$^1/_2$ cup finely chopped fresh parsley
$^1/_4$ cup Mozzarella cheese, grated
1 egg beaten with a dash of white pepper
1 cup vegetable oil (for frying)

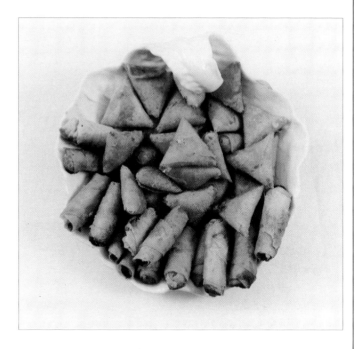

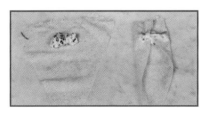

Steps:

1. Soak white cheese in water for 1 night. Change water occasionally. Drain.
2. Spread filo pastries. Cut in half. Place semi-circles over each other. Cut in half in order to get triangles.
3. Filling: Mix all ingredients except the vegetable oil.
4. Put some of the filling in the center of the smooth side of the filo pastries. Fold sides and roll neatly. Brush side with some flour dissolved in $^1/_4$ cup of water to seal.
5. Fry in hot oil until golden. Serve hot with main dishes.

Meat-Cheese-Leek Pastries

Sambusik bilkarrath-jiben-lahem

Sambusik is usually served as an appetizer. It is an important part of meals in the Gulf.

Serves: 4

Preparation time: about 1 hour

Cooking time: about 35 minutes

Ingredients:

5 cups all purpose plain flour
1 ¹/₂ cups lukewarm water
2 tablespoons salt
2 tablespoons sugar
vegetable oil for deep frying
1 cup oil

Cheese filling:
2 cups (425 g/14 oz) white cheese (Ikawi
* Altishiki), grated and salted (p 61)*
¹/₄ cup finely chopped fresh parsley
¹/₄ teaspoon ground cayenne pepper

Meat filling:
300 g (10 oz) ground meat
1 tablespoon shortening or butter
¹/₄ cup fried pine nuts
a dash of ground allspice
¹/₄ teaspoon salt

Leek filling:
¹/₂ cup finely chopped onion
1 tablespoon shortening or butter
1 cup finely chopped leek
¹/₄ teaspoon salt
a dash of pepper

Steps:

1. Prepare dough: see p 12. Cover and leave aside for 1 hour.
2. Cheese filling: Mix ingredients and put aside.
   Meat filling: Fry meat in shortening, add salt, spices and pine nuts. Stir over medium heat for 1 minute. Put aside.
   Leek filling: Fry onion and leek in shortening. Add salt and pepper. Stir for 1 minute. Put aside.
3. Divide dough into walnut-size balls. Roll out to form circles (8 cm diameter).
4. Fill ¹/₃ the circles with cheese, another ¹/₃ with meat and the last ¹/₃ with leek following this way:

Put filling on one side of circle.

5. Fold over one end to make semi-circles.
6. Press edges with fingers.
7. Fry in 1 cup of vegetable oil over medium heat. Brown both sides.
8. Serve hot.

> Note: 1) You can add ¹/₄ cup of chopped onion to meat filling.
> 2) You will get 25 pieces of every kind.

Vegetable Rolls

Rakaek bil khoudar

You can freeze these rolls, defrost and fry before serving.

Serves: 4

Preparation time: about 45 minutes

Cooking time: about 15 minutes

Ingredients:

8 filo pastries
1 cup grated carrots
³/₄ cup grated onions
1 cup thin cabbage strips
1 ¹/₄ cups vegetable oil
¹/₄ teaspoon salt

Steps:

1. Spread filo pastries, cut each in half in order to get 16 peices.
2. Fry all ingredients in ¹/₄ cup of oil for 5 minutes over low heat. Stir. Remove and put aside.
3. Put some vegetable mixture on the smooth side of each filo. Fold sides and roll neatly. Fry in hot oil over medium heat till golden-brown.
4. Serve hot.

Thyme Pastries

Manakeesh bi zahtar

One of the most famous Lebanese pastries.

Serves: 4-6
Preparation time: 60 minutes
Cooking time: 15 minutes

Ingredients:

$^1/_2$ quantity basic dough recipe (exclude oil and add 1 teaspoon yeast dissolved in $^1/_4$ cup of water)
6 tablespoons thyme (zahtar)
$^1/_2$ cup olive oil

Steps:

1. Set oven at (250°C/525°F).
2. Divide dough into rounds. Cover with cloth for 15 minutes. Roll out each round to medium thickness (8 cm diameter) on floured board.
3. Place rounds on greased baking sheet. Mix zahtar and oil together. Spread mixture evenly over the rounds. Bake for 15 minutes in a moderately hot oven (180°C/350°F).
4. Serve for breakfast or for a snack.

Meat Pastries in Yoghurt

Shishbarak

A Lebanese main meal, delicious and nutritious.

Serves: 5
Preparation time (without dough): 1 hour 10 minutes
Cooking time: 20 minutes

Ingredients:

2 kg (64 oz) cooked yoghurt (see p 13)
¹/₂ quantity of basic dough recipe (see p 12)
3 cloves garlic, crushed with a dash of salt
1 cup finely chopped fresh coriander

Filling:
¹/₂ kg (16 oz) ground meat
3 medium sized onions, finely chopped
¹/₄ cup fried pine nuts
1 teaspoon salt
¹/₄ teaspoon ground allspice
¹/₄ teaspoon ground cinnamon
2 tablespoons shortening or butter

Steps:

1. Roll out dough with a rolling pin to about 1 cm thickness.
2. Turn a coffee cup over, press over dough to get equal rounds.
3. Fry onion in shortening till color changes a little. Add meat, salt, allspice and cinnamon. Stir occasionally and fry for 10 minutes. Add pine nuts. Mix. Drain the mixture, butter would affect closing pastries.
4. Spread the round a little with your fingers.

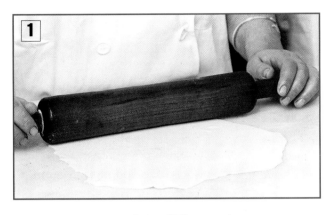

Place 1 teaspoon of the filling on it.

5. Fold over one end to make a semi-circle. Press edges down to seal.

6. Take the two ends from the straight side, bring them together to make a small ring. Press well. Repeat till rounds are done.

7. Place in a tray in a hot oven (200- 250°C/400-525°F) for 10 minutes or until golden.

8. Add to boiling cooked yoghurt (see p.13) one by one. Let it boil over low heat for 10 minutes or till pastries are cooked.

9. Fry with shortening coriander and garlic. Add to cooked yoghurt mixture. Cook another 2 minutes.

10. Serve hot or cold with cooked rice.

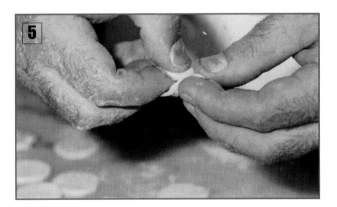

Spinach Pies
Fatayer bi sbanigh

An energetic appetizer.

Makes about: 40
Preparation time: about 45 minutes
Cooking time: 30 minutes

Dough Ingredients:

5 cups all purpose (plain) flour
1 tablespoon sugar
1 tablespoon salt
1 ¹/₂ cups of water
¹/₄ cup vegetable oil

Filling:

1 ¹/₂ kg (48 oz) fresh spinach
¹/₂ cup lemon juice
3 large onions, finely chopped
1 teaspoon salt
1 pinch of ground black pepper
2 tablespoons ground sumac (as desired)
¹/₄ cup vegetable oil
1 tablespoon pomegranate thickened juice (as desired)

Steps:

1. To prepare dough: (see p. 12) leave aside and cover for an hour to rise. Make sure dough doubles in volume.
2. Filling: Remove roots and yellow leaves from spinach. Chop finely then wash well and drain, rub with ¹/₂ teaspoon salt. Drain the spinach again with your hands to dry. Mash the onions with remaining salt. Add pepper and sumac. Add spinach to onion, then mix in oil and pomegranate. Put aside.
3. Roll out dough using a rolling pin till dough is as thin as possible (5 mm). Invert a tea cup on dough and press to have equal circles.
4. Place a tablespoon of spinach filling on each piece.
5. Bring up sides at 3 points to form a triangular shape.
6. Press edges firmly with fingertips to seal completely (put flour on finger tips to help seal).
7. Place pies on oiled baking sheets. Bake in a moderately hot oven (200°C/400°F) for 30 minutes.

Note: You can substitute spinach with unchopped purslane leaves.

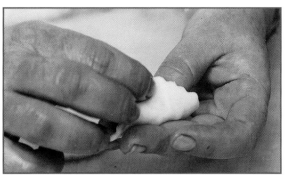

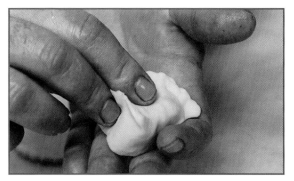

Meat Pastry Rolls

Lahem bi ajeen

Delicious meat pastries.

Makes: about 18
Preparation time: 1 hour
Cooking time: 30 minutes

Ingredients:

3 cups all purpose (plain) flour
1 egg
1 teaspoon salt
³/₄ cup water
4 cups vegetable oil

Filling:

400 g (14 oz) finely minced meat
3 onions, finely chopped
1 teaspoon salt
a dash of Lebanese ground 7 spices
2 tablespoons shortening or butter
2 tablespoons fried pine nuts
1 tablespoon ground sumac
1 tablespoon pomegranate thickened juice (if available)

Steps:

1. Mix flour, egg, salt, and water. Knead well, until dough is firm.
2. Put vegetable oil in a deep tray. Divide dough into small balls (walnut size). Put them in the tray and make sure they are covered with oil. Cover with a piece of texture and leave aside for 4 hours.
3. Fry onion in shortening until golden. Add minced meat, allspice and salt and fry over medium heat for 15 minutes. Stir, fried pine nuts, sumac, and pomegranate juice into meat. Preheat oven (200°C/400°F) for half an hour before you put the pastries.
4. Put one dough ball on an oiled board and spread it using your finger-tips to form a very thin rectangle.
5. Fold to form half a rectangle, then fold from right to left.
6. Place 1 tablespoon of filling across one side of the squares.
7. Fold the other side to cover filling, and press to close.
8. Arrange in an oven tray. Bake at (200°C/400°F) for 30 minutes.
9. Serve hot or cold with yoghurt or salads.

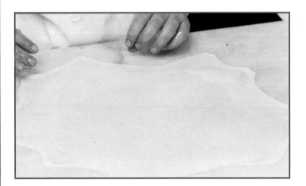

Meat Pastries

Baalbeck sfiha

One of the most famous Lebanese savoury pastries.

Serves: 5
Preparation time: 60 minutes
Cooking time: 30 minutes

Ingredients:

Dough, same recipe (see p. 12 exclude oil and
*   add 1 teaspoon yeast dissolved in $^1/_4$ cup water)*
$^1/_2$ kg (16 oz) ground lamb meat
1 kg (32 oz) firm tomatoes, finely chopped
5 medium onions, finely chopped
1 teaspoon salt
a dash of: ground cayenne red pepper, ground
*   cinnamon, and ground allspice*
2 tablespoons butter, diced
2 tablespoons yoghurt
1 tablespoon sesame paste (Tahinah)
1 tablespoon pomegranate thickened juice (if
*   available)*
4 tablespoons fried pine nuts

Steps:

1. Mix well meat, tomatoes, onion and spices. Add yoghurt, sesame paste and pomegranate. Mix all with fried pine nuts. Add butter.
2. Divide dough into walnut size balls. Roll between hand palms to smooth.
3. Roll out balls with a rolling pin to form 8 cm diameter circles. Put one tablespoon of meat mixture on dough circle seeing that a cube is in each spoon.
4. Bring the edges up and press to make a square.
5. Arrange meat pastries in a tray brushed with butter. Bake in a moderate heat oven (180°C/350°F) for 30 minutes or till dough is golden and meat is cooked.
6. Serve hot with yoghurt.

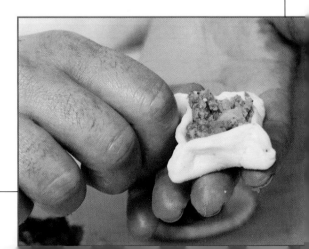

SOUPS

All of us have memories of hot bowls of soup that warmed us during the cold winter days when we were ill. For some of us it was chicken soup, for others spinach soup, for me, it was tomato soup.

Through out our lives, we've always heard that soup is good for us. Nutritionists, now agree with such motherly advice. Indeed a bowl of soup is usually full of nutrients.

According to a study by diet specialists, soup consumed at the beginning of a meal slows the rate of eating. It fills the stomach, which signals the brain to curtail the appetite. As a result, less calories are consumed during the meal.

Soup is the recommended dish to start a main meal with or to have as complete light meal. It is easy to prepare and nutritious. It can be stored in the refrigerator for up to 3 days and reheated.

During Ramadan, fasting month, it is a must to have some soup before starting the meal. Chicken soup, Lentils soup, Vegetable soup, etc. all are wonderful during this holy month.

We have chosen the most delicious soups from all over the Arab world. They adapt without fuss to all types, ranging from hearty family fare to stylish starters for a dinner party. Follow our recipes and see that you have never tried anything like them before.

Vegetable Soup

Hisaa al-khoudar

This soup has a variety of vegetables, added to either meat or chicken. It can be served as an appetizer or a light meal.

Serves: 5
Preparation time: about 40 minutes
Cooking time: 2 hours 30 minutes

Ingredients:

¹/₂ kg (16 oz) chicken or cubed stew lamb meat
1 kg (32 oz) red ripe tomatoes, peeled and finely chopped
1 cup frozen green peas
1 cup cubed carrots
1 cup cubed potatoes
1 cup cubed zucchini
¹/₂ cup finely chopped fresh parsley
1 medium sized onion, peeled
¹/₂ cup roughly chopped string beans
¹/₂ tablespoon salt (as desired)
¹/₄ teaspoon ground black pepper
2 tablespoons butter
¹/₄ cup rice
2 ¹/₂ litres water

Steps:

1. Fry meat in butter until brown.
2. Add meat with onion, spices and salt to a pot filled with water. Cover and simmer for 2 hours or till tender.
3. Add vegetables and rice to meat. Cover and cook on medium heat for 30 minutes.
4. Add parsley. Remove from heat. Serve with main dishes with toasted bread.

Note: If you choose chicken, cook it for 40 minutes then remove bones.

Chicken Soup

Hisaa al dajaj

It is one of the hearty world known soups. All soups keep well, under refrigeration. They retain their full flavor when reheated.

Serves: 6
Preparation time: 20 minutes
Cooking time: 1 hour

Ingredients:

1 kg (32 oz) chicken, cut into 4 pieces
¹/₂ cup broken vermicelli
1 medium sized onion, peeled
2 tablespoons chopped celery or chopped fresh parsley
2 tablespoons shortening or butter
¹/₂ tablespoon salt (as desired)
2 ¹/₂ litres (10 cups) water
2 cinnamon sticks
1 cardamom pod -1 clove -1 nutmeg

Steps:

1. Fry the chicken in shortening for 7 minutes. Add 2 ¹/₂ liters of water, onion and solid spices and cook over medium heat for 40 minutes, or till tender.
2. Remove skin and bones from chicken pieces and cut meat into small cubes. Strain stock. Return cubes to stock.
3. Add celery, vermicelli and salt to stock and bring to a boil.
4. Simmer over low heat for 20 minutes. Serve hot.

Spinach with Fried Kibbi Balls Soup

Hisaa al sbanekh ma akras al-kibbi al moshamaa

A nutritious soup rich with minerals.

Serves: 4
Preparation time: 30 minutes
Cooking time: 30 minutes

Ingredients:

250 g (8 oz) finely chopped trimmed spinach,
* washed and drained*
6 cups water
10 kibbi balls baked for 10 minutes in a moderate
* heat oven (p. 156)*
2 tablespoons finely chopped fresh coriander
1 teaspoon salt
a dash of ground allspice
2 tablespoons shortening or butter
1 medium onion, finely chopped
3 cloves garlic, crushed with a dash of salt
1 tablespoon rice

Steps:

1. Fry onion with shortening until soft. Stir in spinach.
2. Place water in a pot. Add spinach mixture and spices.
3. Stir mixture occasionally until it boils. Add rice. Cook for 15 minutes.
4. Fry garlic and parsley with shortening for 5 minutes. Add to soup.
5. Add kibbi balls to soup. Cook for 5 minutes. Remove from heat. Serve hot.

Tomato Soup

Hisaa al tamatem

A well known soup in the Arab world.

Serves: 6
Preparation time: 30 minutes
Cooking time: 45 minutes

Ingredients:

400 g (14 oz) lean meat, minced
¹/₂ cup chopped parsley
¹/₂ cup broken vermicelli
¹/₂ kg (16 oz) soft red tomatoes, washed and squeezed
1 teaspoon salt
¹/₂ teaspoon ground allspice
2 tablespoons butter
4 cups water

Steps:

1. Mix the meat with half the amount of salt and allspice. Divide into small balls.
2. Fry the meat with shortening over medium heat for 5 minutes.
3. Add water, tomato juice, salt and allspice to meat and cook for ¹/₂ hour or till tender.
4. When it boils, add vermicelli, and simmer for 15 minutes. Add parsley and simmer for 1 minute.
5. Serve it hot.

Lentil Soup

Hisaa al adas

An Arabian hot appetizer.

Serves: 4
Preparation time: 20 minutes
Cooking time: 1 hour 40 minutes

Ingredients:

1 cup brown lentils
2 tablespoons rice
6 cups water
$^1/_2$ teaspoon salt
$^1/_2$ teaspoon ground cumin
$^1/_4$ teaspoon ground allspice
1 medium onion, finely chopped
1 tablespoon shortening or butter or vegetable oil
$^1/_4$ cup finely chopped fresh parsley
1 pitta, toasted and cut into cubes

Steps:

1. Wash lentils and rice well. Place in a pot with water. Bring to a boil. Cover and simmer gently for about $1^1/_2$ hour.
2. Transfer the soup to a food processor or blender. Add 1 cup of water and blend well.
3. Put the mixture in the pot. Simmer over low heat. Add allspice, cumin and salt.
4. Fry the chopped onion till soft. Add to lentil mixture. Bring the mixture to a boil for 10 minutes. Add chopped parsley.
5. Serve soup with toasted bread and lemon wedges.

Sour Lentil Soup

Hisaa al adas bhamud

We advise you to prepare this soup in cold winter days. It is both easy and nutritious.

Serves: 4

Preparation time: 1 hour

Cooking time: 50 minutes

Ingredients:

1¹/₂ cups white lentils, picked stones, washed and drained
¹/₂ kg (16 oz) Swiss chard, trimmed and roughly chopped
1 head garlic, crushed with a dash of salt
¹/₂ cup finely chopped fresh coriander
¹/₂ cup oil or butter
¹/₂ cup lemon juice
4 cups water
1 teaspoon salt
3 medium potatoes, peeled and diced
¹/₄ cup finely chopped onions
1 teaspoon ground cumin

Steps:

1. Put lentils and water in a pot over high heat, bring to a boil. Lower heat, Simmer for 25 minutes.
2. Add Swiss chard and potatoes. Cook over low heat for 15 minutes.
3. Fry onions in oil, then add garlic and coriander, fry till fragrant for about 1 minute.
4. Add garlic mixture, cumin, and lemon juice to lentil mixture. Cook for 10 minutes.
5. Serve hot.

Lentil and Macaroni Soup

Rashta

An Arabian soup, high in protein.

Serves: 6
Preparation time: 20 minutes
Cooking time: 45 minutes

Ingredients:

100 g (4 oz) Macaroni
1 cup white lentils
2 cups finely chopped fresh coriander
6 cloves garlic, crushed with a dash of salt
1 onion, finely chopped, fried till transparent
2 litres of water
¹/₄ cup vegetable oil or shortening
¹/₄ teaspoon ground cumin
1 teaspoon salt (as desired)

Steps:

1. Remove stones and dirt from lentils. Wash, put 2 litres of water in a pot, add lentils and bring to a boil. Cover and cook over low heat for 25 minutes or till tender.
2. Add Macaroni, simmer for 15 minutes. Add onion.
3. Pound coriander, cumin, salt and garlic. Fry this mixture in hot oil, add to lentils mixture. Boil for 2 minutes.
4. Serve hot.

RICE

Rice is the center of every meal for more than half of the world's population. Its cultivation and harvest is the hub of commerce, culture, tradition, superstition, and religion. Although archaeologist disagree about the exact date and place of origin, they do agree that rice is indigenous to Asia.

Tiny grains of rice are so intensely packed with nutrition that it's no wonder more than half the world's people depend on rice for their very survival. In fact, rice alone is capable of supplying 80 percent of the body's daily requirements.

This healthful grain is one of the best sources of complex carbohydrates, the high-energy fuel that powers the body. Rice is also a good source of protein. In addition, rice is easy to digest, cholesterol-free, gluten-free, low in sodium, non allergenic, and contains only a trace of fat.

There are over forty-thousand varieties of rice known to botanists. The familiar varieties of rice are divided into classes according to the length of their grains: short, medium, and long.

Rice is so delicious on its own that it's well worth learning how to cook it perfectly every time. Rice is also very versatile. First, it is blared enough to be the ideal accompaniment to other foods. Second, its juice absorbing priorities render it the best starting point for a wide range of culinary triumphs. The Arabic cooks work magic with this grain, which lead to a large variety of rich rice dishes perfect as a main meal or as the center of a dinner party.

Chicken with Rice

Riz bil dajaj

A main meal of chicken and rice.

Serves: 4

Preparation time: 20 minutes

Cooking time: 1 hour

Ingredients:

1 chicken, about 1 ¹/₂ kg (48 oz)
2 cups long grain rice
400 g (14 oz) minced meat
¹/₄ cup fried pine nuts
¹/₂ cup fried almonds
2 medium sized onions (1 whole, 1 finely chopped)
¹/₄ cup vegetable oil and butter mixture
1 teaspoon ground cinnamon
2 teaspoons salt (as desired)
a dash of ground allspice
2 tablespoons butter
1 cup canned mushrooms (as desired)
1 cardamom pod, 1 nutmeg, 1 clove
2 cinnamon stalks

> *Note: If you desire brown rice see p. 10.*

Steps:

1. Wash the chicken well and cut into 4 pieces.
2. Fry chicken pieces in oil and butter mixture until golden from both sides.
3. Put it in a deep, heavy pan and add to it one peeled onion with 1 teaspoon of salt, cardamom pod, clove, nutmeg and cinnamon sticks.
4. Add 1¹/₂ liters of water, cover and cook over medium heat for 30 minutes. Reserve stock.
5. Fry finely chopped onions in butter, keep stirring till soft and golden.
6. Add minced meat, allspice, cinnamon, and salt to chopped onions and fry for 10 minutes over medium heat.
7. Wash rice and drain, then add to meat and onion. Stir occasionally over low heat for 3 minutes.
8. Add 4 cups of boiling chicken stock to the rice, add mushrooms and cover. Cook rice over high heat for 5 minutes. Lower heat to low and cook for 20 minutes.
9. Pile rice onto large platter with chicken pieces in center and spread over the nuts. Serve hot with cucumber mixed with yoghurt and salad.

Rice with Fresh Broad Beans

Riz bfool akhdar

A main meal served usually with mixed green salad.

Serves: 5
Preparation time: 20 minutes
Cooking time: 45 minutes

Ingredients:

¹/₂ kg (16 oz) minced meat
¹/₂ kg (16 oz) green broad beans, trimmed
2 cups long grain rice
3 ¹/₂ cups water
3 medium onions, finely chopped
1 teaspoon salt
¹/₂ teaspoon ground cinnamon
2 tablespoons butter or shortening
¹/₂ cup fried pine nuts

Steps:

1. Fry onion with butter until soft. Add meat, salt and cinnamon. Cook until meat is brown and tender.
2. Add beans to meat mixture and cook for 5 minutes. Add water and cook over medium heat for 10 minutes.
3. Add rice to pot and bring to a boil for 5 minutes. Cover pot, lower heat, and continue cooking for another 20 minutes or until rice is tender.

Note: If you desire the rice to be brown look at page 10.

83

Prawns and Rice

Riz bil kraydis

Another delicious Saudi Arabian main meal.

Serves: 5
Preparation time: 20 minutes
Cooking time: 45 minutes

Ingredients:

¹/₂ kg (16 oz) uncooked prawns, cleaned
2 cups long grain rice, washed and drained
¹/₄ cup frozen green peas
¹/₄ cup finely chopped carrots
1 teaspoon salt
¹/₄ teaspoon ground saffron
1 teaspoon grated green ginger or ¹/₄ teaspoon
  ground dried ginger
¹/₄ teaspoon ground piquant pepper
1 large onion, finely chopped
2 cloves garlic, crushed with a dash of salt
¹/₄ cup vegetable oil

Steps:

1. Fry prawns in oil for 5 minutes over high heat. Remove from heat and put on absorbent paper. Add all ingredients except rice to pot, stirring constantly for 2 minutes.
2. Add 1 liter water and bring to a boil for 10 minutes over moderate heat.
3. Add rice and see that water is covering mixture. If not, add some.
4. Cook for 15 minutes then lower heat, cook for another 10 minutes until rice is cooked. Stir in prawns until cooked.
5. Serve hot with sesame paste dip (see p.11).

Rice with Truffles

Riz bil laham wa alkima

A hearty and satisfying dish for a cold winter day.

Serves: 5
Preparation time: 30 minutes
Cooking time: 2 $^1/_2$ hours

Ingredients:

1 kg (32 oz) truffles
1 small onion, finely chopped
3 cups long grain rice, washed and drained
400 g (14 oz) minced meat
600 g (20 oz) stew meat, diced
3 tablespoons shortening or butter
a dash of salt (as desired)
a dash of ground cinnamon
a dash of ground pepper
1 cup fried pine nuts and almonds (for garnishing)
1 litre (4 cups) water
1 tablespoon salt (for cleaning truffles)

Steps:

1. Soak truffles in cold water for 15 minutes. Peel using a sharp knife.
2. Put one litre of water and salt in a pot. Add truffles, bring to a boil. Chop into medium size pieces.
3. Sauté stew pieces with shortening until golden. Place aside.
4. Sauté stew meat with a dash of salt in the same shortening. Transfer meat to another pot. Add 2 litres of water to the pot and cook for 2 hours. Reserve stock.
5. Sauté onion with the same shortening on medium heat until transparent. Add minced meat, cinnamon, pepper, and salt to onion. Cook until meat is brown and tender.
6. Use 6 cups of stock to cook rice. Add rice to stock. Cover pot. Bring to a boil for 5 minutes. Reduce heat and cook for 20 minutes.
7. Spoon rice into a platter. Top with truffles, minced meat, and stew meat. Garnish with fried pine nuts and almonds.

Biryani Rice

Riz biryani

A Saudi classic, perfect for lunches, buffets, and suppers alike.

Serves: 5
Preparation time: 30 minutes
Cooking time: about 1 hour

Ingredients:

$^1/_2$ kg (16 oz) shoulder meat, cubed
2 cups long grain rice (Basmati), washed
$^3/_4$ cup chopped onion
2 tablespoons shortening or butter
$^1/_4$ teaspoon saffron threads, soaked in $^1/_4$ cup of water
1 teaspoon ground dried coriander
1 teaspoon ground cinnamon
1 teaspoon ground ginger
1 teaspoon cumin seeds
4 cups chicken stock
salt (as desired)
2 bay leaves
$^1/_4$ teaspoon ground clove
$^1/_2$ teaspoon ground nutmeg
$^1/_2$ cup finely chopped fresh coriander
2 tablespoons butter
$^1/_2$ cup fried onion rings, for garnish
60 g (2 oz) roasted cashew nuts
$^1/_2$ cup seeded raisins

Steps:

1. Heat shortening in a pot over low heat. Stir in onions until golden.
2. Stir in meat. Add coriander (dried and fresh), bay leaves, and spices (except saffron). Stir until meat becomes golden.
3. Remove bay leaves. Add salt, saffron, chicken stock, and rice to the same pot (stock level should be 5 cm higher than rice level). Add butter. Cover pot. Cook over low heat until tender (and the water evaporates).
4. Mix mixture with a spoon. To serve, line a large serving platter with rice-meat mixture, sprinkle fried onion rings, cashew nuts and sultanas. Serve hot

Rice with Vegetables

Riz maa khoudar

It is a side-dish, served with fish or meat.

Serves: 3
Preparation : 20 minutes
Cooking time: 45 minutes

Ingredients:

2 cups long grain rice
1 cup finely chopped carrots
1 cup frozen green peas
300 g (10 oz) minced meat
1/2 cup blanched and fried almonds
4 cups chicken or meat stock (or water)
2 tablespoons shortening (butter)
Salt (as desired)
a dash of cinnamon and pepper

Steps:

1. Place shortening in a pot over medium heat, fry minced meat with spices until tender, then add carrots till soft.
2. Add peas, salt and stock. Bring to a boil. Cook for 20 minutes.
3. Add rice and cover. Cook for 5 minutes. Reduce heat to low and cook for another 20 minutes.
4. Serve garnished with almonds.

Saudi Arabian Rice and Meat

Kapse

Kapsé, is a Saudi Arabian main meal.

Serves: 10
Preparation time: 45 minutes
Cooking time: 2 hours 30 minutes

Ingredients:

2 ½ kg (60 oz) lamb leg or shoulder meat, large
    cubes
4 cups long grain rice
½ kg (16 oz) carrots, peeled and finely chopped
1 green pepper, seeded and finely chopped
½ kg (16 oz) green peas
1 kg (32 oz) red tomatoes, peeled and chopped
1 kg (32 oz) finely chopped onion
1 medium sized garlic head, peeled and crushed
½ teaspoon ground saffron
¼ teaspoon ground cardamom
½ teaspoon ground cinnamon
½ teaspoon ground allspice
¼ teaspoon ground white pepper
1 tablespoon salt
shortening for frying
Fried almonds and pine nuts for garnishing

Steps:

1. Fry meat pieces till brown from both sides. Cover with water, bring to a boil then cook gently over medium heat for 2 hours or till tender. Reserve stock.
2. Soak rice for 15 minutes. Drain, wash well, then drain again.
3. Add shortening to a pot, fry on medium heat all ingredients except rice and meat. Cook on low heat for about 10 minutes, or until tender.
4. Add rice to vegetables in the pot, stir fry for 4 minutes on medium heat. Add stock meat until the stock covers the rice. Cover pot. Cook on low heat for 30 minutes or until tender.
5. Serve rice in a large platter. Garnish with meat, almonds, and pine nuts.

Sauce:

Ingredients:

2 cups meat stock
1 large onion, peeled and finely chopped
2 large tomatoes, peeled and finely chopped
2 cloves garlic, peeled and crushed
1 tablespoon tomato paste
¼ cup chopped celery
1 teaspoon salt (as desired)
1 teaspoon cinnamon
2 tablespoons shortening

Steps:

1. Fry onion, garlic and tomato in shortening. Add tomato paste, salt, cinnamon and meat stock.
2. Cook mixture on medium heat. When it thickens, add celery.
3. Serve the sauce beside the Kapsé platter.

Overturned Eggplant

Makloubat al bathinjan

Casseroles are ideal for the cook who likes to entertain, because they usually demand a minimum of last-minute attention and can be assembled in advance.

Serves: 5
Preparation time: 15 minutes
Cooking time: 45 minutes

Ingredients:

2 cups long grain rice, washed and drained
1/2 kg (16 oz) minced meat
1 medium onion, peeled and finely chopped
1 kg (32 oz) medium round eggplants
2 tablespoons shortening or butter (for frying meat and onion)
4 cups vegetable oil (for frying eggplants)
1/2 cup fried pinenuts and almonds
1/4 teaspoon ground allspice
1/4 teaspoon ground cinnamon
1/4 teaspoon ground black pepper
4 cups water

Steps:

1. Peel eggplants. Chop lengthwise into 1 cm thick slices. Sprinkle some salt over eggplants and leave aside for 1 hour. Fry eggplants in oil, remove and drain on absorbant paper.
2. Sauté onion with shortening until transparent over medium heat. Stir in meat, salt, and spices. Cook until meat is brown and tender.
3. Arrange in layers in a pot: 1/4 quantity meat, eggplants, remaining meat and rice. Add gradually water.
4. Place pot over moderate heat. Boil for 5 minutes. Lower heat and cook for 20 minutes or until water evaporates. Turn over pot into a large plate (larger than pot).
5. Sprinkle fried pine nuts and fried almonds on top of the eggplants. Serve hot accompanied with yoghurt and salads.

GRAINS

Lentils, dried peas, and beans are all pulses, or seeds from the pods of certain leguminous plants. They are excellent foods to include in your diet. They have very little fat, no cholesterol, and substantial amounts of protein. Most importantly, they offer a good fiber content, high in water-soluble fiber, which helps remove cholesterol from the body, in a similar way to oat bran.

The initial step of presoaking beans often deters people from using dried beans. Lentils are the most convenient, requiring no presoaking to soften before cooking. Alternatively, canned beans are quick and nutritious. There is some loss of B vitamins during canning, but this is not significant. A couple of cans of beans in your cupboard is always handy for an easy, no fuss high fiber meal.

They are unobtrusive stars, easy to use, wonderfully filling and economical too. The pulses style is shown in hearty main meals, dinner party fare, casual lunches and snacks, all with lots of color and great taste. Often we have blended various grains and pulses together for variety and texture.

On the other hand, grains such as wheat have been the staple food of many people for centuries and for good reason. In fact, all are high in complex carbohydrate and fiber, with a good protein content and very little fat or salt. They are nourishing, satisfying foods that we should all include in generous quantities in our diet.

Start exploring the fabulous range of grains with us, and see how readily they blend with other ingredients in a great variety of enticing dishes. Choosing from our flavorsome versions of favorite recipes, you'll have no difficulty enjoying these delicious foods each week.

Burghul with Meat

Burghul bil dpheen

It is an Arabian main meal that is served with yoghurt and salad.

Serves: 4

Preparation time: 45 minutes

Cooking time: 30 minutes

Ingredients:

1 cup coarse burghul, washed well and drained
¹/₂ cup canned chickpeas, washed and drained
500 g (16 oz) lamb stew meat, cubed
500g (16 oz) small onions, peeled
2 tablespoons shortening or butter
¹/₄ teaspoon ground allspice
¹/₂ teaspoon ground cinnamon
¹/₄ teaspoon ground caraway
2 cups water
1 teaspoon salt (as desired)
Fried pine nuts (for garnishing)

Steps:

1. Fry meat with 1 tablespoon of shortening. Cover with water. Cook for 2 hours. Remove scum as it appears.
2. Fry onion with shortening and with a dash of salt and caraway until soft. Add chickpeas and 2 cups of water. Cook on medium heat for 5 minutes.
3. Stir-fry burghul in the remaining shortening on medium heat for 5 minutes.
4. Add to burghul 1 cup of meat's stock, 1 cup of onion's stock, and the remaining spices. Cook all on medium heat until they boil. Lower heat and cook for 20 minutes or until tender.
5. Serve in a platter, garnished with lamb pieces, onion, pine nuts, and chickpeas.

Note: You can combine meat stock with onion stock and serve beside burghul with meat. If you want stock to be thick add 1 tablespoon of cornflour dissolved in some water.

Burghul with Tomato

Burghul bil tamatim

A side-dish, easy to prepare and economical. If you wish to serve alone, accompany with yoghurt and salad.

Serves: 5

Preparation time: 20 minutes

Cooking time: 30 minutes

Ingredients:

2 cups coarse burghul, washed well and drained
¹/₂ cup finely chopped onion
1 tablespoon vegetable oil or shortening
1 kg (32 oz) tomatoes, peeled and roughly chopped
1 teaspoon of salt
¹/₂ cup water
a dash of allspice
a dash of cinnamon
a dash of red pepper (as desired)

Steps:

1. Fry onions over low heat till soft.
2. Add tomatoes, water, salt, and spices and bring to a boil over medium heat.
3. Add burghul, liquid must cover, so add more water if needed.
4. Cook over medium heat for 10 minutes or till water evaporates. Keep covered.
5. Cook over low heat for 15 minutes or till burghul is cooked.
6. Serve hot.

Note: You can add 2 finely chopped green bell peppers by frying them with onion in step 1.

Burghul Pilaf

Burghul m'falfal

It is usually served with stews as a substitute for cooked rice.

Serves: 4

Preparation time: 10 minutes

Cooking time: 30 minutes

Ingredients:

2 ¹/₂ cups coarse burghul
1 teaspoon salt
¹/₄ teaspoon ground pepper
4 cups water
¹/₄ cup butter
¹/₂ cup crumbled fine vermicelli

Steps:

1. Fry vermicelli in heated butter in a pot. Add burghul. Fry for 5 minutes over moderate heat.
2. Stir in salt, pepper and water. Bring to a boil. Lower heat and cover pot. Continue cooking for 20-25 minutes.
3. Serve hot when burghul becomes fluffy and moist.

Lentils with Dough

Harra isbau bil-ajeen

A very delicious Syrian appetizer.

Serves: 5
Preparation time: 1 hour
Cooking time: 1 hour 30 minutes

Ingredients:

1 ¹/₂ cups brown lentils
8 cups water
1 ¹/₂ cups all purpose flour
2 large onions, chopped (¹/₂ cup)
1 cup finely chopped fresh coriander
¹/₂ cup lemon juice
1 cup olive oil
2 tablespoons pomegranate thickened juice
1 head garlic, crushed with a dash of salt
¹/₂ cup vegetable oil
¹/₂ teaspoon of salt
a dash of ground allspice

Dough Steps:

1. Put flour with ¹/₂ cup of water and some salt in a bowl. Knead dough and leave for 2 hours then sprinkle flour over it.
2. Roll out the dough on a floured surface, till it becomes as thin as possible and round shaped. Fold about 7 cm at one end. Sprinkle flour and fold another 7 cm, same side. Repeat until dough is all layers.
3. Cut dough into small squares then open them. Put half the quantity in a flat dish. Fry the other half in ¹/₄ cup of hot vegetable oil until golden. Use to garnish at the end.

Steps:

1. Pick small stones or dirt from lentils then wash lentils well, and place in a heavy pan with water. Bring to a boil. Cook on medium heat for 1 ¹/₂ hours or until tender. Add lemon juice, pomegranate juice, olive oil, salt, and pepper. Mix well.
2. Fry sliced onions with ¹/₄ cup of vegetable oil until golden. Add half the quantity of onions to the lentils.
3. Fry in vegetable oil crushed garlic, coriander and add half the quantity to the lentils.
4. Add unfried dough squares to lentil mixture. Keep stirring till dough is cooked (about 20 minutes).
5. Serve hot or cold, garnished with fried onions, coriander and fried dough pieces.

Grilled Wheat Grains

Freekeh

A delicious Syrian dish of grilled wheat grains with meat.

Serves: 5

Preparation time: about 45 minutes

Cooking time: 3 hours

Ingredients:

400 g (14 oz) lamb stew meat, cubed
2 cups freekeh (grilled green wheat)
1 medium sized onion, peeled
2 tablespoons shortening or butter
1 teaspoon salt
¹/₂ teaspoon ground cinnamon
¹/₂ cup pine nuts fried in vegetable oil
¹/₂ cup blanched and fried almonds
some fat

Steps:

1. Fry meat with 1 tablespoon shortening till brown all over.
2. Cover with water, add peeled onion, salt, cinnamon, cook over medium heat for 2 hours or till tender.
3. Remove meat, put aside. Reserve stock.
4. Remove stones from freekeh, wash and drain. Fry freekeh with fat and shortening.
5. Bring stock to a boil, adjust salt. Add freekeh and see that stock is about 7 cm above freekeh.
6. Bring to a boil over medium heat. Reduce heat and cook for 30 minutes (don't stir mixture).
7. Serve it garnished with meat, almonds and pine nuts.

Potato and Burghul Kibbi

Kibbi healeh

A new way of preparing kibbi from potato and burghul.

Serves: 5
Preparation time: 30 minutes
Cooking time: 45 minutes

Ingredients:

3 cups smooth burghul
2 medium potatoes
a dash of ground coriander
a dash of ground cumin
a bunch of fresh coriander, finely chopped
1 teaspoon salt
¹/₂ kg (16 oz) onion, peeled and sliced
1 tablespoon pomegranate thickened juice
a dash of ground turmeric
¹/₂ cup vegetable oil

Steps:

1. Boil potatoes until cooked. Peel and process using a manual processor. Soak burghul for 10 minutes. Wash and drain well.
2. Knead burghul with potatoes, salt, and half the quantity of spices (except turmeric) into a smooth dough.
3. Fry onion rings, salt, and remaining spices in some oil. Stir in turmeric and pomegranate juice on moderate heat until soft.
4. First way: Spread potato and burghul dough onto a baking tray like baked meat kibbi (p.172). Second way: Divide potato dough into egg sized balls. Smooth balls with wet palms. Make a hole in the middle with your forefinger. Work finger round in the hole until you have a shell of even thickness. Fry in hot oil until golden. Place on absorbent paper. When cool, fill with onion filling.
5. Serve accompanied with vegetable salad.

Couscous

A Moroccan main meal, suitable to prepare when you have a gathering, yet you don't want to stay long in the kitchen.

Serves: 4

Preparation time: about 30 minutes

Cooking time: 1 hour

Ingredients:

1 packet of couscous (about 2 cups)
1 chicken quartered
1 large onion, cut into 4 pieces
$^1\!/_2$ teaspoon salt
2 tablespoons shortening or butter
2 cinnamon sticks
$^1\!/_4$ cup shortening (or butter) and vegetable oil mixture
200 g (7 oz) chopped and fried sausages
2 cups water
1 teaspoon oil (for cooking couscous)
1 clove -1 nutmeg- 1 cardamom pod
raisins for garnishing

Steps:

1. Fry chicken with shortening and oil mixture.
2. Cover chicken, onion, and solid spices with 2 litres of water. Cook over medium heat for 1 hour or until the chicken is tender. Remove chicken and place aside.
3. Boil water. Add salt, oil, couscous, and butter. Turn heat off.
4. Mix using a fork until couscous absorbs all the water. Leave aside for 7 minutes (you can reheat the couscous on low heat while stirring constantly).
5. Remove couscous from water. Drain. Place in a platter, garnish with chicken, raisins, and sausages.

Couscous Sauce:

200 g (7 oz) stew meat (lamb's leg), cubed
1 medium green pepper, chopped (into small pieces)
3 medium carrots, peeled and chopped into circles
3 medium zucchini, washed and chopped into medium pieces
200g (7 oz) string beans, washed
1 medium potato, peeled and cut into medium pieces

5 cabbage leaves, washed and finely chopped
1/2 cup finely chopped onion
5 garlic cloves, crushed with a dash of salt
1/2 cup finely chopped coriander
1 cup tomato juice
1/2 teaspoon salt
2 tablespoons butter
1 tablespoon flour
a dash of allspice
a dash of ground white pepper

Steps:

1. Fry meat with butter and with a dash of salt and allspice for 10 minutes.
2. Add 1 litre of water to the pot. Cover and cook on medium heat for 2 hours or until meat is tender.
3. Add all remaining ingredients to meat and stock. Cook on low heat for 30 minutes or until vegetables are tender.
4. Serve hot beside couscous.

Orange Lentils Purée

Mjadra bayda

A popular dish, which is high in protein.

Serves: 5
Preparation time: 10 minutes
Cooking time: 1 hour

Ingredients:

1 ¹/₂ cups of red split lentils
¹/₂ cup rice
¹/₂ cup vegetable oil
6 cups of water
1 medium sized onion, finely chopped
1 teaspoon salt (as desired)

Steps:

1. Remove stones and dirt from lentils, wash and drain. Put oil in a pot over medium heat, add onion and stir till transparent. Add lentils and rice. Stir for 3 minutes.
2. Add water and cover pot. Bring the mixture to a boil, then simmer over low heat for 1 hour, stirring occasionally. When mixture thickens, mix in salt.
3. Serve hot with mixed green salad.

Strained Lentils

Mjadra msaffaye

A meatless dish. It is both nutritious and filling.

Serves: 4
Preparation time: 30 minutes
Cooking time: 2 hours

Ingredients:

1 ¹/₂ cups brown lentils, picked stones, washed, drained
¹/₂ cup rice, soaked for 1 hour
¹/₂ cup vegetable oil
¹/₂ cup finely chopped onion
1 teaspoon salt

Steps:

1. Put lentils in a pot, cover with water, bring to a boil over high heat. Cover. Simmer for 1 hour and 30 minutes till cooked.
2. Process with liquid into a purée.
3. Put lentil purée in a pot, add rice, salt and 1 cup water. Cover. Cook over medium heat for 10 minutes.
4. Fry onions. Add to lentil mixture. Lower heat. Cook for 15 minutes till rice is tender.
5. Pour in serving bowls. Serve cold with salads.

Lentils with Rice

Mdardra

An Arabian meatless meal.

Serves: 5
Preparation time: 15 minutes
Cooking time: 1 hour

Ingredients:

1 cup white lentils
2 cups long grain rice
4 medium onions, peeled and sliced lengthwise, fried
¼ cup vegetable oil
1 teaspoon salt
4 cups water

Steps:

1. Remove stones and dirt from lentils then wash.
2. Put water in a pot. Add lentils. Bring to a boil over medium heat, then reduce heat and cook for 25 minutes or till tender with pot covered.
3. Add rice and salt, if water isn't double the quantity of rice and lentils, add more water.
4. Cover and boil over low heat for 30 minutes.
5. Garnish with onions and serve with yoghurt-cucumber salad.

Moughrabiyya

It consists of very tiny dumplings. You can say it is a big size Couscous.

Serves: 5

Preparation time: 30 minutes

Cooking time: 1¹/₂ hours

Ingredients:

1 kg (32 oz) Moughrabiyya packet
1 chicken (1 kg/32 oz), quartered
¹/₂ kg (16 oz) stew meat, cubed
1 cup canned chickpeas, washed and drained
1 kg (32 oz) small onions, peeled
2 teaspoons ground caraway
1 large onion, peeled and finely chopped
2 teaspoons ground cinnamon
2 teaspoons salt (as desired)
a dash of ground allspice
a dash of white pepper
2 tablespoons shortening or butter (for frying moughrabiyya)
2 tablespoons shortening (for frying meat and chicken)
8 cups water
¹/₂ teaspoon oil

Steps:

1. Fry meat with shortening until golden-brown. Stir in chopped onion, half teaspoon salt and a dash of all-spice. Remove meat and place in a pot. Add 8 cups of water. Cover and cook for 2 hours. Add small onions and half quantity of spices. Cook for 10 minutes. Add ¹/₂ quantity of chickpeas and cook for 2 minutes.
2. Fry chicken with same shortening. Add a dash of salt, white pepper, and some water. Cover and cook on medium heat for 45 minutes or until tender.
3. Cook moughrabiyya dumpling in a pot of salted boiling water with oil for 10 minutes. Remove pot from heat. Pour moughrabiyya in a colander and wash under cold running water.
4. Fry moughrabiyya dumpling with a dash of salt and shortening in a large pot on medium heat. Add gradually meat stock until dumplings are soft. Add remaining spices, salt, and remaining chickpeas to dumpling. Mix well.
5. Pour some meat stock over moughrabiyya dumplings. Mix well. Place aside some onions for garnishing.
6. Serve in a large platter. Garnish with chicken pieces and small onions. Sprinkle over some cinnamon.
7. Serve hot accompanied with meat's stock.

Lima Bean Stew

Yakhnet al fasoulia

When you have a yearning for grandma's real home cooking, try this recipe.

Serves: 5
Preparation time: 20 minutes
Cooking time: 2 hours 40 minutes

Ingredients:

$^1/_2$ kg (16 oz) dried or fresh lima beans, soaked in water for one night
400 g (14 oz) stewing meat, cubed
2 cups tomato juice
3 tablespoons shortening or butter
1 tablespoon salt
a dash of ground allspice
6 cloves garlic, crushed with $^1/_2$ cup finely chopped coriander

Steps:

1. Fry meat with 1 tablespoon of shortening until golden-brown. Put meat in a generous quantity of water in a pot. Cook over medium heat for 2 hours.
2. Cook beans in double its amount of salted water. Remove and drain.
3. Fry beans in the remaining shortening for 3 minutes. Add meat, meat's stock, tomato juice, salt, and allspice. Cover and cook for 30 minutes (add water if necessary).
4. Fry coriander and garlic till fragrant for 2 minutes. Add to beans mixture. Cook for 1 minute.
5. Serve beans hot, accompanied with cooked rice.

VEGETABLES

If you enjoy eating well, you will enjoy this section. Eating the right food is essential to your total health.

That is why vegetables are vital to your diet. They add crunch, color and vitality to your food. They have no cholesterol or fat; they are packed with vitamins, minerals and fiber. Also they are so low in kilojoules (calories) that you can eat them quite freely; and the type of fiber they contain helps lower cholesterol.

In a triumph of tastes and textures, we have used a fabulous range of vegetables for recipes selected from all over the Arab world. They are innovative without being difficult, giving you new ways with favorites, plus the chance to try something you might not have thought of using, such as Jew's Mallow (Melokia) and okra.

Vegetables are fantastic to work with because they are easy to handle, mix and match brilliantly with all kinds of tantalizing ingredients. You'll also find a colorful variety of vegetable dishes, with and without meat.

Tasting these dishes is an experience not to be missed. And when you tempt your tastebuds with our light, refreshing selection of vegetable recipes, you can safely come back for a second helping.

Taro with Sesame Paste

Aranbiyet al-kolkas

A new way of preparing taro.

Serves: 5

Preparation time: 1 hour

Cooking time: 25 minutes

Ingredients:

1 kg (32 oz) taro
Aranbiyeh sauce (see kibbi balls with sesame
* paste page 174)*
¹/₄ cup fried pine nuts
¹/₂ cup vegetable oil

Steps:

1. Cook taro covered with water for 5 minutes. Peel and chop into medium pieces.
2. Sprinkle salt on taro pieces, leave aside for 30 minutes. Wash under warm water several times to get rid of the jelly material that appears. Drain well.
3. Fry taro in oil on low heat until slightly golden, remove and place on absorbent paper.
4. Add taro pieces into prepared aranbiyeh sauce. Cook on low heat for 20 minutes or until tender.
5. Serve hot beside rice pilaf; garnish with fried pine nuts.

Artichoke with Meat

Ardi chawki bil lahem

A very tasty dish perfect for all occasions.

Serves: 6
Preparation time: 30 minutes
Cooking time: 1 hour 15 minutes

Ingredients:

12 artichoke heads
400 g (14 oz) minced meat
1 medium onion, finely chopped
¹/₂ cup fried pine nuts
2 tablespoons butter for frying meat and onion
¹/₂ teaspoon salt
¹/₄ cup lemon juice
1 cup finely chopped boiled carrots (optional)
a dash of ground pepper
a dash of ground allspice
a dash of flour
2 cups water for cooking artichokes

Steps:

1. Cover artichoke heads with water, flour and lemon juice. Boil for 10 minutes. Remove and fry in some butter. Place aside.
2. Fry onion until soft. Stir in meat, salt, and spice. Cook on low heat for 15 minutes, stirring occasionally.
3. Remove meat from heat. Stir in carrots.
4. Distribute meat mixture over prepared artichokes. Place in a tray. Add water. Cover and cook over moderate heat for 15 minutes or until tender.
5. Serve artichokes hot, garnished with pine nuts and accompanied by cooked rice, radishes and lemon.

Okra with Meat

Bamia bil lahem

This dish is delicious and easy to prepare specially if you use canned or frozen okra.

Serves: 5

Preparation time: 30 minutes

Cooking time: 2 hours 30 minutes

Ingredients:

1 kg (32 oz) fresh small okra (if large cut in half, crosswise), rinsed, top pointed, stem peeled (not cut) off

400 g (14 oz) stew meat, cubed

1 kg (32 oz) tomatoes, peeled and chopped

1 ¹/₂ cups water

¹/₂ tablespoon salt

¹/₂ teaspoon ground allspice

¹/₂ teaspoon ground cinnamon

2 tablespoons butter or shortening

1 small onion, finely chopped

1 head garlic, peeled and crushed with a dash of salt

a bunch of green coriander, finely chopped

1 lemon, squeezed

Steps:

1. Sauté stew meat with shortening. Place meat in another pot. Cover with water. Add salt. Cover and cook for 2 hours. Place aside.
2. Sauté onion with shortening until transparent.
3. Stir in okra for 8 minutes.
4. Stir in garlic and coriander for another 3 minutes.
5. Add tomatoes, meat, stock, lemon juice and spices.
6. Shake the pot twice on moderate heat. Cover and cook for 25 minutes.
7. Serve hot accompanied with rice.

Baked Stuffed Vegetables

Khoudar mahshua bil forn

This main dish is good for all occasions.

Serves: 5
Preparation time: 1 hour
Cooking time: 30 minutes

Ingredients:

5 medium potatoes, peeled
4 small tomatoes, slightly cored from bottom
$^1/_2$ kg (16 oz) small eggplants, peeled
$^1/_2$ kg (16 oz) small zucchini
5 hearts artichoke (canned)
1 medium sweet green bell pepper, cored from
  bottom
$^1/_2$ kg (16 oz) small carrots, cut into rounds
$^1/_4$ cup lemon juice (unsweetened)
$1^1/_2$ cups vegetable oil for frying vegetables
$^1/_4$ teaspoon salt

Filling:

750 g (24 oz) minced lamb or beef meat
1 large onion, finely chopped
$^1/_2$ cup fried pine nuts
1 teaspoon salt
$^1/_2$ teaspoon ground cinnamon
2 tablespoons shortening or butter

Note: You can also cook stuffed vegetables over moderate heat gas until it boils then lower heat and cook for 30 minutes or until tender.

Steps:

1. Core potatoes. Fry in oil until golden. Remove and put aside.
2. Cut eggplants and zucchini stems. Slit once lengthwise each. Fry eggplants, zucchini, and artichokes until golden. Remove and place aside.
3. Fry carrots in same oil until golden. Put aside.
4. Filling: Sauté onion with shortening on medium heat until transparent. Stir in meat, salt and cinnamon until tender. Remove from heat.
5. Mix meat with pine nuts. Stuff vegetables accordingly.
6. Arrange in an oven tray keeping carrots in the middle.
7. Dissolve salt in 2 cups of water and pour with lemon juice over vegetables.
8. Cover tray. Bake in a moderate heat oven (180°C/350°F) for 30 minutes or until tender.
9. Serve hot with cooked rice.

Stuffed Gourds and Eggplants

Kareh wa bathinjan mahshowan

A main meal, served with green onions and fresh mint. You can follow the same recipe and substitute gourds and eggplants for baby marrow.

Serves: 4

Preparation time: about 1 hour

Cooking time: about 2 hours

Ingredients:

750 g (24 oz) small gourds (if small is unavailable cut the large into 4 pieces crosswise)
750g (24 oz) purple black, long eggplants
1/2 cup short grain rice
500 g (16 oz) minced meat
1 head garlic, peeled and crushed with a dash of salt
1/2 kg (16 oz) tomatoes, peeled and finely chopped
1/2 teaspoon ground dried mint
1 tablespoon lemon juice
a dash of ground black pepper and ground cinnamon
1 tablespoon shortening or vegetable oil
1/2 tablespoon salt (as desired)
1/4 cup finely chopped onion

Steps:

1. Peel gourds.
2. Roll eggplants on a smooth surface.
3. Remove stems.
4. Core with a special corer, wash and drain.
5. Filling: Mix meat, onion, rice and season well.
6. Stuff eggplants and gourds. Don't overstuff.
7. Arrange in a pot. Sprinkle salt. Add tomatoes, garlic, mint, lemon juice, shortening and water to cover. Cook over high heat. Bring to a boil.
8. Reduce heat. Cook till tender for about 2 hours. Serve hot.

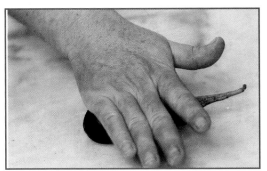

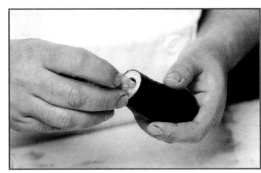

Mixed Vegetables

Khoudra mshakle (mousabahet aldarweish)

A famous main dish of vegetables and meat.

Serves: 5
Preparation time: 1 hour
Cooking time: 2 hours 30 minutes

Ingredients:

600 g (20 oz) boneless lamb leg or shoulder (cubed)
¹/₂ kg (16 oz) carrots
¹/₂ kg (16 oz) zucchini
¹/₂ kg (16 oz) eggplants
¹/₂ kg (16 oz) potatoes
1 kg (32 oz) tomatoes
4 medium onions, finely chopped
¹/₄ cup lemon juice
1 tablespoon salt
a dash of ground pepper
a dash of ground cinnamon
3 tablespoons shortening or butter
1¹/₂ liters water

Steps:

1. Peel eggplants, carrots, potatoes and wash well, then cut into cubes.
2. Wash zucchini and cut into cubes.
3. Peel tomatoes and finely chop them.
4. Fry meat with 2 tablespoons of shortening with half the quantity of salt and spices. Cover with water and cook over moderate heat for 2 hours with pot covered. Place aside.
5. Sauté onion with remaining shortening until transparent. Stir in carrots for 5 minutes. Add zucchini and stir for 3 minutes.
6. Add tomatoes with 1 cup of water to carrot's mixture. Cook over low heat for 10 minutes.
7. Add eggplant and cook for 10 minutes. Add fried potatoes and remaining salt and pepper.
8. Add meat and stock to cover. Cover pot and cook for 30 minutes or until tender.
9. Serve hot with green bell pepper and spring onion.

Lebanese Stuffed Zucchini

Kousa ablama

The Mediterraneans like stuffed vegetables, when it comes to zucchini, you have a big variety of recipes. They might look the same but each has its special taste. Try this recipe, it is different!

Serves: 5

Preparation time: 1¹/₂ hours

Cooking time: 45 minutes

Ingredients:

1 kg (32 oz) small zucchini
300 g (10 oz) minced meat
¹/₂ cup finely chopped onion
3 cloves garlic, peeled and crushed with a dash of salt
¹/₂ teaspoon dried mint
1 teaspoon salt
¹/₄ teaspoon ground black pepper
¹/₄ teaspoon ground cinnamon
¹/₂ cup fried pine nuts
1 tablespoon pomegranate thickened juice
¹/₄ cup lemon juice
4 tablespoons shortening or butter
2 ¹/₂ cups water

Steps:

1. Core zucchini using an apple corer. Wash well.
2. Fry onion with half the quantity of shortening until transparent. Add minced meat and spices and fry for 10 minutes or until tender. Add pine nuts. Mix well.
3. Stuff zucchini with meat mixture. Fry with remaining shortening and place on absorbent paper.
4. Add zucchini to a pot. Add water, garlic, mint, pomegranate juice and lemon juice. Cover pot. Cook over medium heat for 30 minutes.
5. Serve hot accompanied by cooked rice.

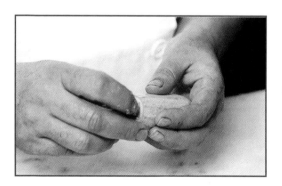

Stuffed Zucchini with Yoghurt

Kousa mahshu bil laban

A main meal for those who like yoghurt.

Serves: 5
Preparation time: 1 hour
Cooking time: 50 minutes

Ingredients:

2 kg (64 oz) zucchini, medium size
1 ¹/₂ kg (46 oz) yoghurt
3 cloves garlic, crushed with a dash of salt
leaves of 5 mint stalks, finely chopped
4 cups water
¹/₂ teaspoon salt (as desired)

Filling:
¹/₂ kg (16 oz) ground meat
1 ¹/₂ cups rice
2 tablespoons shortening or butter
a dash of salt
¹/₄ teaspoon ground cinnamon
¹/₄ cup fried pine nuts (optional)

Steps:

1. Cook yoghurt (see p. 13).
2. Wash zucchini, cut off stem and hollow them with an apple corer.
3. Mix all ingredients of filling.
4. Stuff zucchini. Put in a pot with water, salt, and ¹/₄ the quantity of cooked yoghurt. Cook over medium heat for 30 minutes.
5. Add zucchini to boiling yoghurt, cook over medium heat for 15 minutes. Add crushed garlic with dried mint to mixture. Boil for another 5 minutes.
6. Serve with spring onions and fresh mint.

Green Bean Stew

Yakhnet lubya

A famous stew, usually served with cooked rice and tomato-onion salad seasoned with lemon juice, crushed garlic and olive oil.

Serves: 4
Preparation time: about 35 minutes
Cooking time: about 45 minutes

Ingredients:

1 kg (32 oz) green beans, string, snip off the ends, snip each into two, wash and drain
750 g (24 oz) stew lamb cutlets
1/2 teaspoon ground pepper
2 tablespoons shortening or butter
1 teaspoon salt
3 cups water

Steps:

1. Fry meat with shortening over medium heat till brown. Season.
2. Stir in green beans for 15 minutes on low heat.
3. Add water, salt and pepper. Cover and cook on medium heat until boiling.
4. Lower heat. Continue cooking until beans are tender. Serve hot accompanied by cooked rice.

Stuffed Zucchini in Tomato Sauce

Kousa mahshou bil-tamatem

A famous dish in the Arab world.

Serves: 5
Preparation time: about 40 minutes
Cooking time: 1 hour

Ingredients:

1 kg (32 oz) medium zucchini
200 g (7 oz) minced meat
1 cup short grain rice, washed
1 kg (32 oz) red tomatoes, peeled and chopped
2 teaspoons salt
a dash of ground allspice and black pepper (as desired)
a dash of ground cinnamon (as desired)
1 tablespoon shortening or butter
5 cloves garlic, crushed with a dash of salt
2 cups water
4 tablespoons lemon juice

Steps:

1. Wash well zucchini. Remove stems using a knife. Hollow out using an apple corer. Wash zucchini inside and out. Drain.
2. Filling: Mix minced meat with rice. Stir in salt and spices.
3. Stuff zucchini, shake each after filling it so that the filling is well distributed (don't over stuff). Arrange in a pot. Invert a plate on top.
4. Strain tomatoes using a colander. Add 2 cups of water, shortening, and a dash of salt. Place tomato juice in a pot over medium heat. When it boils, add to zucchini. Cook for 1 hour, or until tender. Add crushed garlic and lemon juice. Cook for 5 minutes.
5. Serve zucchini and sauce hot separately or together in a large bowl.

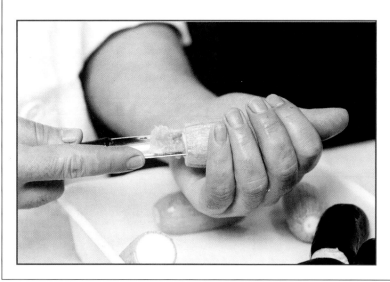

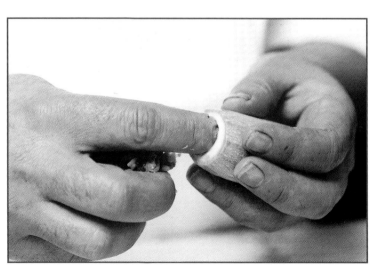

Syrian Stuffed Zucchini in Yoghurt

Sheikh al mahshi bil-kousa

A Syrian national dish.

Serves: 5
Preparation time: 30 minutes
Cooking time: 1 hour

Ingredients:

1 ¹/₂ kg (46 oz) small zucchini
600 g (21 oz) minced meat
3 tablespoons fried pine nuts
1 cup water
1 cup shortening or butter
Salt and pepper (as desired)
2 kg (64 oz) cooked yoghurt (see p. 13)

Steps:

1. Wash well zucchini. Remove stems with a sharp knife. Hollow zucchini with an apple corer. Wash inside and out. Drain.
2. Fry zucchini with shortening until golden. Place aside. Fry minced meat with a dash of salt and pepper until tender. Mix half the quantity of pine nuts with minced meat.
3. Stuff zucchini with meat (don't over stuff), shake to spread the filling. Arrange stuffed zucchini in a pot. Pour 1 cup water. Cook on low heat for 15 minutes.
4. Add stuffed zucchini to cooked yoghurt. Cook on medium heat for 30 minutes.
5. Place stuffed zucchini and yoghurt in serving plates. Sprinkle on top the minced meat and pine nuts. Serve accompanied with cooked rice.

Lebanese Jew's Mallow

Melokhia lebnaneya

A Lebanese main meal of herbs with meat and chicken.

Serves: 5
Preparation time: 1 hour
Cooking time: 3 hours

Ingredients:

¹/₂ kg (16 oz) of fresh Jew's mallow (melokhia) leaves

1 kg (32 oz) chicken, cleaned quartered

600 g (20 oz) lamb stew meat, cubed

1 large onion, peeled

1 cup fresh coriander, finely chopped

3 heads garlic, peeled

¹/₄ cup ground dried coriander

1 tablespoon salt (as desired)

3 tablespoons shortening or butter

3 tablespoons shortening or butter (for frying jew's mallow)

a dash of ground white pepper, cinnamon, and black pepper

Steps:

1. Fry meat with 2 tablespoons of shortening and a dash of salt, cinnamon, and black pepper. Remove and place in another pot. Cover with water and cook over moderate heat. Bring to a boil then lower heat, cover pot, and continue cooking for 2 hours until tender.

2. Fry chicken with same shortening and a dash of salt and white pepper on low heat. Cover with water. Cover pot and cook on moderate heat for 45 minutes. Remove and put aside.

3. Grill onion. Process onion with dried coriander, one peeled head of garlic, and a dash of salt. Put aside.

4. Fry jew's mallow in batches with shortening. Remove and place aside.

5. Fry remaining garlic and onion mixture with remaining shortening. Stir in coriander and jew's mallow leaves. Add meat and stock.

6. Cover pot and cook over low heat for 1 hour until tender.

7. Serve hot garnished with chicken and a dash of cinnamon accompanied by cooked rice, radishes, and lemon.

Egyptian Jew's Mallow

Melokhia masriya

Jew's mallow is a long leafy vegetable which you might find only dried.

Serves: 6
Preparation time: 1 hour
Cooking time: 1 hour

Ingredients:

1 kg (32 oz) fresh picked jew's mallow leaves, finely chopped or
¹/₂ kg (16 oz) dried leaves soaked in boiling water for 1 hour
2 medium chickens, cleaned and quartered
1 tablespoon salt
1 cup finely chopped fresh coriander
1 tablespoon ground dried coriander
¹/₄ cup olive oil
4 heads garlic, peeled
1 large onion, peeled
2 cinnamon sticks
1 nutmeg - 1 clove - 1 cardamom pod

Steps:

1. Put chicken in a large pot, cover with water. Add onion, salt and solid spices. Bring to a boil. Cook over medium heat for 1 hour. Bone the chicken and put aside.
2. Crush 1 peeled head of garlic with a dash of salt and coriander (dried and green). Fry 3 heads of garlic and coriander mixture in oil over low heat for 3 minutes.
3. Put 1 ¹/₂ liters of strained boiling stock in a clean pot. Add Jew's mallow and garlic mixture. Boil for 5 minutes.
4. Serve in a large bowl accompanied with chicken. It is optional to serve 1 cup of vinegar mixed with 2 finely chopped onions, toasted bread and chili. A little of these ingredients is added to every plate.

Pea with Carrots Stew

Yakhnit al bazila maa al jazar

*Through out the world peas are cooked in
different ways. This is one of the good stew
recipes.*

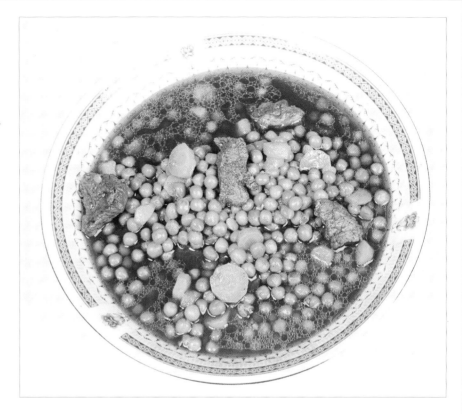

Serves: 4

Preparation time: 20 minutes

Cooking time: 2 hours 20 minutes

Ingredients:

1 kg (32 oz) green peas (frozen)
$^1/_2$ kg (16 oz) lamb or beef stew meat, cubed
$^1/_2$ kg (16 oz) carrots, peeled and chopped
1 teaspoon salt (as desired)
a dash of ground allspice
a dash of ground cinnamon
1 $^1/_2$ tablespoons tomato paste
4 cups of water
3 tablespoons shortening or butter

Steps:

1. Fry meat with 1$^1/_2$ tablespoons butter until
   golden. Add spices and water. Cover pot and
   cook for 2 hours until tender.
2. Fry carrots in remaining butter for 3 minutes on
   low heat. Stir in peas then tomato paste.
3. Add meat to peas. Cover with stock. Cover pot.
   Cook on low heat for 20 minutes.
4. Serve hot with cooked rice.

*Note: You can substitute tomato paste with garlic and
coriander mixture.*

Swiss Chard Leaves Stuffed with Meat

Warak al solk al mahshou bil lahem

A famous winter dish.

Serves: 4
Preparation time: 40 minutes
Cooking time: 50 minutes

Ingredients:

1¹/₂ kg (48 oz) Swiss chard
1 cup short grain rice
400 g (14 oz) minced meat
¹/₂ cup lemon juice
¹/₄ cup shortening or butter
1 teaspoon salt
a dash of ground paprika
a dash of ground cinnamon
3 cups water

Steps:

1. Remove Swiss chard roots. Blanch leaves in boiling water for few seconds. Remove with slotted spoon and put in cold water, then place in a colander. Repeat the same procedure with remaining leaves.
2. Mix rice with minced meat, spices and salt.
3. Place a Swiss chard leaf, shiny side down, on a work surface. Cut into 2 or 3 pieces (depending on size of leaf).
4. Place crosswise about a tablespoon of stuffing (depending on the size of leaf).

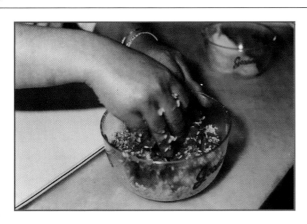

5. Fold ends and roll firmly. Repeat with remaining leaves.
6. Place ¹/₂ cup of shortening in a heavy pan. Pack leaf rolls close together in layers. Invert a heavy plate on top to keep rolls in shape during cooking.
7. Add lemon juice, 3 cups of water, and a dash of salt. Place pan over moderate heat, bring to a boil. Lower heat and cook for 45 minutes or until tender.
8. Serve hot accompanied with cooked Swiss chard stems in sesame paste.

Cabbage Leaves Stuffed with Meat

Warak al malfouf al mahshou bil lahem

A nutritious main dish.

Serves: 4
Preparation time: 40 minutes
Cooking time: 2 hours

Ingredients:

1 ¹/₂ kg (48 oz) cabbage
1 cup short grain rice
400 g (14 oz) minced meat
¹/₄ cup lemon juice (as desired)
¹/₄ cup shortening or butter
¹/₄ cup Seville orange juice
1 teaspoon salt
a dash of ground paprika
a dash of ground cinnamon
a dash of ground cumin
3 cups water
1 medium head crushed garlic
¹/₂ teaspoon dried mint (as desired)
1 tablespoon pomegranate thickened juice

Steps:

1. Peel off cabbage leaves. Blanch some leaves in boiling water for few minutes. Remove with a slotted spoon and put in cold water then put in a colander. Repeat same procedure with remaining leaves.
2. Mix rice with minced meat, spices and salt.
3. Place cabbage leaf, shiny side down, on a work surface. Cut into 2 or 3 pieces (depending on size of leaf).
4. Place crosswise about a tablespoon of stuffing (depending on the size of leaf), and fold ends.
5. Roll firmly and repeat procedure with remaining leaves.
6. Place ¹/₂ cup of butter in a pot. Pack leaf rolls close together in layers. Invert a heavy plate on top to keep rolls in shape during cooking.
7. Add to pot lemon juice, Seville orange juice, 3 cups of water, pomegranate juice, garlic, dry mint, and a dash of salt. Bring to a boil on moderate heat. Cover pot. Cook on low heat for 2 hours or until tender (add water if evaporated).
8. Serve hot accompanied by radishes.

Note: you can add some stuffed zucchini.

124

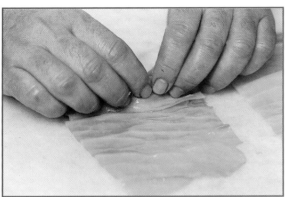
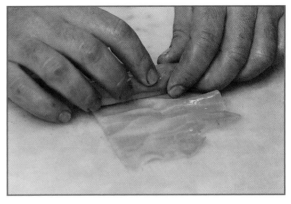

Stuffed Vine Leaves and Zucchini

Warak inab wa kousa mahshuwan

A famous main meal, perfect for a special occasion. Make extra and have them for lunch the next day.

Serves: 8

Preparation time: 1 hour

Cooking time: 2 hours

Ingredients:

1 kg (32 oz) lamb cutlets, fried with shortening or butter
1/2 kg (16 oz) vine leaves, trimmed
1 kg (32 oz) small zucchini
750 g (24 oz) ground meat
1 1/4 cups rice
1/4 teaspoon ground black pepper
1 cup lemon juice
1 head garlic, peeled
1 teaspoon salt (as desired)

Steps:

1. Trim vine leaves. Wash.
2. Pour water in a pot. Bring to a boil.
3. Dip vine leaves in boiling water and lift immediately. Place in cold water then drain.
4. Prepare stuffing by mixing: rice, ground meat, salt and pepper.
5. Spread each vine leaf, shiny side down on a work surface. Put 1 tablespoon / or teaspoon (depending on size of leaf) stuffing on each leaf.
6. Fold sides and roll up into a small and neat roll.
7. Repeat with remaining ingredients.
8. Arrange cutlets in the pot, pack vine leaf rolls close together in layers with garlic cloves in between.

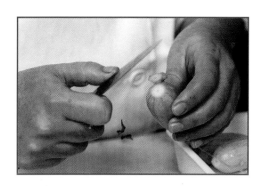

9. Invert a heavy plate on top to keep rolls in shape during cooking.
10. Wash zucchini and cut the stems.
11. Hollow zucchini using an apple corer. Wash from inside and out.
12. Stuff zucchini, not over filling them. Arrange zucchini on top of plate.
13. Add hot water to cover and lemon juice. Bring to a boil.
14. Cover and simmer gently over low heat for 2 hours or until leaves are tender (when cooking add some hot water if necessary to have stock left when served).
15. Arrange in a platter and serve with fresh mint and green onions.

Note: You can prepare steps 1-12 the day before cooking. Place in refrigerator for the next day.

Eggplant Stew

Yakhnet bathinjan

As you notice, onion is an essential ingredient in the Arabian kitchen. This dish gets its special taste from it.

Serves: 4

Preparation time: about 1 hour

Cooking time: about 2 hours

Ingredients:

500 g (16 oz) black eggplants, peeled, cubed
600 g (20 oz) lamb stew meat, cubed
1 cup finely chopped onion
1 tablespoon salt
a dash of ground black pepper and allspice
vegetable oil
1 tablespoon butter or shortening

Steps:

1. Sprinkle salt on eggplant cubes. Place aside for 1 hour.
2. Fry eggplant cubes in hot oil. Remove and drain on absorbent paper.
3. Fry chopped onion for 2 minutes then sauté meat with 2 tablespoons of butter. Cover with water, add salt and spices, and cook on high heat. Bring to a boil. Cover pot and cook on medium heat for 2 hours.
4. Add fried eggplants to meat and stock. Cover pot and cook for 10 minutes.
5. Serve eggplant stew with lemon wedges and eggplant dip.

Potato Stew

Yakhnet batata

It is a delicious dish. Although potato is cooked in many ways, I'm sure you've never tasted something like this before.

Serve: 4
Preparation time: 20 minutes
Cooking time: 2 hours 25 minutes

Ingredients:

1 ¹/₂ kg (46 oz) potatoes, peeled, washed, cubed
600 g (20 oz) lamb stew meat, cubed
1 head garlic, peeled, crushed with a dash of salt
2 ¹/₄ tablespoons shortening or butter
1 ¹/₂ cups vegetable oil (for frying)
1 ¹/₄ cups finely chopped fresh coriander
³/₄ tablespoon salt (as desired)
a dash of ground allspice and black pepper
6 cups water

Steps:

1. Fry potato cubes in hot oil over medium heat till golden. Remove and drain on absorbent paper. Fry meat with 2 tablespoons of butter. Place meat in a pot. Add water. Bring to a boil over high heat. Cover. Reduce heat to low, remove scum when necessary. Cook for 2 hours till meat is tender.
2. Fry coriander and garlic with remaining butter over low heat. Stir till fragrant for about 2 minutes.
3. Add fried potatoes, salt, allspice and pepper to meat and stock. Bring to a boil over medium heat. Reduce heat. Cover. Cook for 15 minutes.
4. Lower heat. Add coriander and garlic. Cook for 5 minutes.
5. Serve hot with cooked rice.

Spinach Stew

Yakhnet sabanegh

One of the many Arabian stews.

Serves: 4
Preparation time: 40 minutes
Cooking time: 20 minutes

Ingredients:

1 kg (32 oz) spinach, washed, stalks removed,
  roughly chopped
¹/₄ kg (8 oz) lean lamb or beef, minced or cubed
2 medium onions, chopped
2 tablespoons shortening or butter
1 tablespoon salt (as desired)
a dash of ground allspice
¹/₄ cup fried pine nuts
4 cloves garlic, peeled and crushed with a dash of
  salt
¹/₂ cup finely chopped fresh coriander
1 liter water

Steps:

1. Boil water in a pot. Add bicarbonate of sodium then chopped spinach. Bring to a boil for 3 minutes. Remove and wash well. Drain. Put aside.
2. Sauté onion with shortening or butter over moderate heat until transparent. Stir in meat, salt and allspice until tender.
3. Stir in garlic then add coriander and spinach. Mix well. Add 1 cup of water. Cook over moderate heat for 20 minutes or until tender.
4. Garnish with pine nuts. Serve accompanied with cooked rice.

Tomato Stew

Yakhnet al tamatem

*A unique main meal. To get the
desired taste, you are advised to use
fresh tomatoes.*

Serves: 4

Preparation time: 30 minutes

Cooking time: 2 hours 20 minutes

Ingredients:

1 kg (32 oz) stew meat, diced
2 kg (64 oz) ripe tomatoes, peeled, diced
*¹/₂ kg (16 oz) eggplants, peeled, cut into long
  thick pieces*
1 medium potato, peeled and cubed
¹/₂ cup fried pine nuts
3 tablespoons shortening or butter
¹/₂ cup vegetable oil
1 teaspoon salt
¹/₂ teaspoon ground cinnamon

Steps:

1. Put half the shortening in a pot, fry meat till
   brown, add 1 liter of water, salt and cinnamon
   and bring mixture to a boil. Let it simmer for 2
   hours or till meat is tender.
2. Fry potato in oil until golden. Remove and put
   on absorbent paper.
3. Sprinkle salt on eggplant pieces. Place aside for
   1 hour.
4. Fry eggplants in hot oil till brown. Drain on
   absorbent paper towels.
5. When stock is reduced to half, add tomatoes,
   potatoes and eggplants. Cover and simmer over
   low heat till stock thickens. Adjust salt according to your taste.
6. Garnish with fried pine nuts. Serve hot with
   cooked rice.

POULTRY

Four and a half millennia ago, the red jungle fowl of southeast Asia, the ancestor of the modern chicken, was domesticated. Four and a half millennia have yielded us an abundance of chickens and numerous ways of serving mankind's favorite fowl.

Today chicken is no longer considered a luxury. Easily prepared, widely available and reasonably priced, it graces tables throughout the world. No other meat can be cooked in as many interesting ways: baking, barbecuing, boiling, frying, grilling, roasting, sautéing, simmering, steaming, and stewing. Chicken can be casseroled, souped, and stuffed. All this makes chicken reigns as one of the most versatile main-dish ingredients you can buy.

This book gives you basic information on buying, cleaning, cutting, boning, and trussing chicken and basic cooking methods.

In addition to providing inspiration and good food, I hope this book helps you develop a new sense of economy in the kitchen. Next time you want to sauté or fry chicken pieces, for example select a whole fresh bird from a quality butcher or poultry shop instead of the prepackaged pieces you might usually buy in a supermarket.

In that spirit, we chose the best dishes from all around the Arab world to please your taste.

Stuffed Pigeons

Al Hamam al mahshu

Egyptians are known for their delicious pigeon recipes. Try this recipe.

Serves: 4
Preparation time: 30 minutes
Cooking time: 1 hour

Ingredients:

8 pigeons, cleaned
200 g (7 oz) ground meat
$^1/_2$ cup rice
$^1/_4$ cup fried pine nuts
$^1/_2$ cup blanched and fried almonds
$^1/_4$ cup blanched and fried pistachio nuts
1 large onion, sliced into rings
$^1/_4$ teaspoon ground cinnamon
1 tablespoon shortening
butter
1 tablespoon salt (as desired)
$^1/_4$ teaspoon ground black pepper
2 bay leaves
4 cardamom pods

Steps:

1. Rub pigeons inside and out with $^1/_2$ quantity of salt and ground spices.
2. Fry meat in shortening. Add $^1/_4$ teaspoon salt and remaining ground spices. Mix for 5 minutes. Add $^1/_2$ cup of water.
3. Add rice to meat. Stir once. Cook on low heat until the water evaporates and the rice is half cooked.
4. Mix rice and meat with pistachio nuts, almonds, and pine nuts. Stuff pigeons (don't over stuff). Stitch opening.
5. Place pigeons in a pot. Add bay leaves, cardamom pods, onion, and 2 cups of water. Cook over medium heat for 5 minutes. Remove scum as it appears. Add salt. Cover pot. Cook on low heat for 45 minutes.
6. Remove pigeons from stock. Brush with butter. Place in a hot oven (220°C/450°F) for 15 minutes until golden.
7. Arrange in platter. Serve hot.

Grilled Pigeons

Al Hamam al mashwi

Pigeons when grilled are delicious. Just take care not to overcook them.

Serves: 4

Preparation time: 20 minutes

Cooking time: about 45 minutes

Ingredients:

8 pigeons (each 500 g/16 oz) cleaned
melted butter
1 tablespoon salt (as desired)
¹/₂ teaspoon ground white pepper

Steps:

1 Rub pigeons inside and out with salt and pepper. Brush with butter.
2 Place in an oven tray. Bake in a moderate heat oven (180°C/350°F) till tender and browned for about 45 minutes.
3 Serve hot with Hummus bi-tahini (see p.33).

Pigeons with Cracked Wheat

Hamam bil-fireek

We chose for you one of the best Saudi Arabian recipes. It is a national dish: delicious and nutritious.

Serves: 4

Preparation time: 35 minutes

Cooking time: 1 hour 25 minutes

Ingredients:

4 pigeons, cleaned
1 tablespoon ground cinnamon
¹/₂ cup butter
2 cups fireek (grilled green wheat), washed and drained
1 teaspoon ground black pepper (as desired)
¹/₄ cup finely chopped onion
¹/₃ cup fat
¹/₂ tablespoon ground cardamon
1 ¹/₂ tablespoons salt (as desired)
3 cups water
¹/₂ cup fried pine nuts
4 tablespoons flour

Steps:

1. Melt some fat with half the quantity of butter in a pan on medium heat. Fry onion in the butter mixture until soft. Stir in fireek for 5 minutes on low heat. Add water and spices. After 15 minutes, remove half the quantity of fireek. Place aside. Cook the remaining half for another 15 minutes or until water evaporates.
2. Rub pigeons with flour and some spices. Stuff pigeons with half the quantity of fireek. Stitch opening. Place pigeons in a pot. Cover with water. Bring to a boil. Lower heat. Cover pot and cook for 40 minutes.
3. Remove pigeons and drain from stock. Place on an oven tray. Brush pigeons with butter. Place tray in moderate heat oven (180°C/350°F). Cook for 20 minutes until pigeons are golden-brown.
4. Serve the remaining fireek in a platter. Place pigeons over fireek. Garnish with pine nuts.

Stuffed Chicken

Al Dajaj al mahshu

A main meal good for special occasions.

Serves: 4

Preparation time: 1 hour 15 minutes

Cooking time: nearly 1 hour

Ingredients:

1 kg (32 oz) chicken, cleaned
¹/₄ cup pine nuts, fried
¹/₄ cup blanched almonds, fried
¹/₄ cup blanched pistachio nuts, fried
200 g (7 oz) minced meat
¹/₄ cup shortening or butter
butter
¹/₄ teaspoon of: ground allspice, ground cinnamon
and ground cardamon
1 tablespoon salt
³/₄ cup long grain rice, washed
1 bay leaf

Steps:

1. Put the minced meat with shortening in the cooking pot, add ¹/₄ teaspoon of salt and ¹/₂ the quantity of the spices. Stir the mixture for 5 minutes, add 1 cup of water.
2. Add the rice to the meat and stir once. Leave it over moderate heat for 15 minutes.
3. Rub the chicken with the remaining spices inside and out.
4. Filling: Mix the cooked rice with pine nuts, almonds and pistachio nuts. Stuff the chicken with the mixture and stitch the opening.
5. Put the chicken on its back in a pot, add the bay leaf and cover with water. Leave over moderate heat, bring to a boil and add a dash of salt. Cover the pot and simmer for 40 minutes (remove scum as it appears).
6. Rub chicken with butter, put in an oven tray on high heat for 15 minutes, till brown and cooked.
7. Serve the chicken with bread and garnished with parsley.

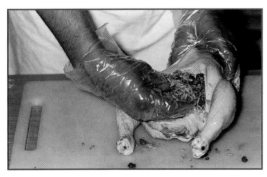

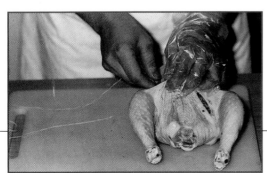

137

Chicken with Paprika

Al dajaj bil shakshouka

A Moroccan savory dish. The sauce that accompanies it makes all the difference in taste.

Serves: 4
Preparation time: 30 minutes
Cooking time: 1 hour

Ingredients:

750 g (24 oz) chicken, quartered
1/4 cup finely chopped onion
2 cloves garlic, crushed
1/4 cup shortening or butter
1 cup finely chopped fresh coriander
1 teaspoon salt (as desired)
1 1/2 cups water
1/2 teaspoon ground black pepper (as desired)

Sauce (Shakshouka):
750 g (24 oz) tomatoes, peeled and finely chopped
750 g (24 oz) green bell peppers, grilled, peeled, finely chopped
1 cup finely chopped parsley
1 cup finely chopped coriander
4 cloves garlic, crushed with a dash of salt
1/2 teaspoon ground chili (as desired)
1/2 teaspoon ground cumin
1/2 teaspoon ground allspice (as desired)
1 teaspoon salt (as desired)
1/2 teaspoon ground black pepper (as desired)

Steps:

1. Fry onions with shortening in a pot over medium heat. Add chicken, coriander, garlic, salt, black pepper and water. Stir, cover and cook for 45 minutes or till tender.
2. Sauce: Mix green pepper, tomatoes, garlic, coriander, and parsley. Fry, stirring, over medium heat for 30 minutes. Add allspice, black pepper, salt, cumin and chili. Bring to a boil. Cook till thick.
3. Serve fried chicken with sauce.

Stuffed Boned Chicken

Dajaj mosahab mahshou

A delicious dish for boned and stuffed chicken breasts lovers.

Serves: 4

Preparation time: about 1 hour

Cooking time: about 1 hour

Ingredients:

*4 boned chicken breasts (keep the bone on the
  wing for garnishing)*
³/₄ cup long grain rice
300 g (10 oz) minced meat
2 tablespoons fried pine nuts
3 tablespoons fried pistachio nuts
¹/₂ cup shortening (or butter)
¹/₃ cup frozen peas
*¹/₂ teaspoon of each: salt, ground cinnamon, all-
  spice, saffron, cardamom*

Steps:

1. Rub chicken from inside and out with ¹/₂ quantity of spices.
2. Fry minced meat with shortening until tender. Stir in for 5 minutes peas, salt, and the remaining spices. Add 2 cups of water. Mix well.
3. Add rice to meat mixture. Cook on low heat for 25 minutes. Put aside.
4. Add pistachio and pine nuts to rice. Mix well. Stuff breasts with rice mixture. Stitch the opening.
5. Rub stuffed breasts with butter. Place stuffed breasts in a high heat oven (220°C/450°F) for 45 minutes or until golden and tender.
6. Serve stuffed breasts garnished with almonds accompanied by vegetable salad.

Barbecued Boned Chicken

Shish tawook

Children love them at lunches and dinners.

Serves: 4
Preparation time: 30 minutes
Cooking time: 30 minutes

Ingredients:

1 kg (32 oz) boned chicken
1 tablespoon ketchup
1 tablespoon tomato paste
1 teaspoon salt
¹/₄ teaspoon ground white pepper
a dash of ground ginger
5 cloves garlic, crushed
³/₄ cup lemon juice
¹/₂ cup vegetable oil

Steps:

1. Mix all ingredients above. Soak for 24 hours in the refrigerator.
2. Place in an oven tray. Place tray in a (220°C/450°F) oven for 30 minutes. Lower heat, cook for 30 minutes or until tender (or thread chicken pieces onto skewers, alternate with mushrooms if desired).
3. Serve accompanied with french fries and garlic purée.

Chicken Shawarma

Shawarma al dajaj

A new way of preparing shawarma.

Serves: 8
Preparation time: 30 minutes
Cooking time: 45 minutes
Soaking time: 24 hours

Ingredients:

2 kg (64 oz) boned chicken, cut into finger size
  slices
2 cups lemon juice
1 ¹/₂ cups vegetable oil
a dash of salt (as desired)
a dash of ground white pepper
a dash of ground paprika
a dash of ground mastic
1 tablespoon ground 7 spices

Steps:

1. Mix all ingredients above. Soak placed in the refrigerator for 24 hours.
2. Place in an oven tray. Enter the tray into a (220°C/450°F) oven for 45 minutes.
3. Serve accompanied with grilled tomatoes, french fries, and salads.

Chicken with Vegetables

Al dajaj maa al khoudar

A world wide known and loved dish.

Serves: 4
Preparation time: 30 minutes
Cooking time: about 1 hour

Ingredients:

1 chicken cleaned and cut into 4 pieces
¹/₂ kg (16 oz) carrots, cooked and cut into circles
¹/₂ kg (16 oz) zucchini, cooked and cut into slices
* (lengthwise)*
¹/₂ cup canned mushrooms
¹/₄ cup cooked green peas
1 large onion, sliced
5 cloves garlic, crushed
¹/₄ cup vegetable oil and butter mixture
¹/₄ cup butter
¹/₂ cup lemon juice
4 cups water
¹/₂ tablespoon salt
¹/₂ teaspoon ground allspice
2 bay leaves
some chopped thyme leaves

Steps:

1. Fry chicken pieces with oil and butter until golden. Remove and place aside.
2. Fry garlic in half the quantity of butter. Add lemon juice, salt, allspice, water, bay leaves, and thyme. Bring to a boil on medium heat.
3. Add chicken pieces. Cook on low heat for 45 minutes. Remove and place on a large platter (reserve 2 cups of chicken stock to make chicken sauce).
4. Fry cooked vegetables in the remaining butter. Garnish chicken with vegetables. Serve hot accompanied with chicken sauce.

Chicken Sauce:

Ingredients:

2 cups chicken stock
1 medium onion
3 cloves garlic
1 carrot, peeled and
   chopped (into circles)
2 bay leaves

1 tablespoon cornflour
2 chopped celery stalks
$1/4$ cup chopped leek
1 tablespoon butter
a dash of salt
a dash of ground white pepper
2 cinnamon sticks

Steps:

1. Place all ingredients (except cornflour and butter) in a pot. Cook on moderate heat for 20 minutes. Remove bay leaves and cinnamon sticks.
2. Remove stock mixture from heat. Process. Return to pot.
3. Dissolve cornflour in some water. Add to processed mixture. Cook on low heat. Stir constantly until it boils.
4. Add butter (as desired), cook sauce until it thickens.

Stuffed Turkey

Al Deek al roomi mahshu

A delicious stuffed turkey. The filling is special, when cooked you'll have a lovely dish.

Serves: 6
Preparation time: 30 minutes
Cooking time: 3 hours

Ingredients:

1 Turkey (about 5 kg/16 oz) cleaned
750 g (24 oz) ground meat
2 cups short grain rice
1 cup finely chopped onion
15 chestnuts, boiled and peeled
¹/₂ cup blanched and toasted almonds
¹/₄ cup fried seedless raisins
1 kg (32 oz) baby potatoes, boiled and peeled
4 cinnamon sticks
¹/₂ teaspoon cardamom pods
1 tablespoon ground black pepper
¹/₂ tablespoon ground cinnamon
¹/₂ tablespoon ground cumin
¹/₂ cup butter
2 tablespoons shortening (or butter)
1 tablespoon salt (as desired)
2 bay leaves

Steps:

1. Rub Turkey inside and out with ¹/₂ quantity of salt, black pepper and ground cinnamon. Put aside.
2. Fry onions with shortening over medium heat, stirring, add ground meat with a dash of salt, black pepper, cumin. Stir occasionally till meat is tender.
3. Add rice, water to cover, bring to a boil, when half cooked remove from pot.
4. Add almonds, raisins, and ¹/₂ quantity of chestnuts to meat mixture. Mix well. Stuff the turkey. Stitch the opening. Place in a large pot. Add cinnamon sticks, cardamom, and bay leaves. Add water to cover. Cook over high heat. When it boils reduce heat to low. Cover and cook for 1¹/₂ hours.
5. Remove from pot. Brush with butter. Place in a deep oven tray. Pour stock over. Bake in a moderate oven till tender and stock almost evaporates (cover with aluminum foil when too brown).
6. Serve in a platter surrounded with extra chestnuts.

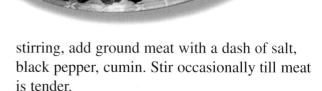

Garlic Chicken on Skewers

Shish tawook magraby

Chicken cooked in this manner is a light main course. These skewers can also be baked in a moderate oven.

Serves: 4
Preparation time: 20 minutes
Grilling time: 30 minutes
Soaking time: 1 hour

Ingredients:

500 g (16 oz) boneless, skinless chicken, cut into strips
3 cloves garlic, crushed with a dash of salt
¹/₄ cup vegetable oil
¹/₂ tablespoon salt (as desired)
¹/₂ teaspoon ground black pepper
¹/₂ teaspoon ground cumin
¹/₂ cup finely chopped fresh parsley

Steps:

1. Mix well chicken, garlic, parsley, pepper, cumin, salt and oil in a bowl. Cover and put aside for 1 hour.
2. Thread into skewers. Grill on an outdoor grill, keep turning till brown and tender.
3. Serve with garlic purée.

Note: If you use wooden skewers, soak them in water for 1 hour before using.

Chicken With Almonds

Dajaj bil loz

A delicious Moroccan dish.

Serves: 5
Preparation time: 30 minutes
Cooking time: 60 minutes

Ingredients:

5 boneless, chicken breasts
1 cup fried almonds
¹/₄ cup chopped mushrooms, canned
¹/₄ cup finely chopped celery
1 ¹/₂ cups grated mozzarella cheese
1 cup milk
1 tablespoon flour
1 teaspoon salt
¹/₄ cup butter

Steps:

1. Melt butter in a pot. Add flour then milk.
2. Mix mushrooms with celery, salt, grated cheese, and almonds. Add mushroom mixture to flour mixture. Mix well.
3. Stuff each chicken piece with 1 tablespoon or more of stuffing. Stitch well.
4. Brush each piece with some butter. Arrange in a greased oven tray. Place in a moderate heat oven (180°C/350°F) for 1 hour or until tender.
5. Serve hot accompanied with chicken sauce (p. 143), boiled vegetables and cooked rice.

Fried Sparrows

Al asafir al mouhammara

Small birds are very tasty specially when cooked the right way. This is one of the good recipes.

Serves: 4
Preparation time: 20 minutes
Cooking time: 30 minutes

Ingredients:

8 sparrows, cleaned/or any game birds
$^1/_2$ teaspoon salt
$^1/_4$ cup lemon juice
1 tablespoon pomegranate thickened juice
1 tablespoon butter
a dash of white pepper

Steps:

1. Fry sparrows in butter over medium heat till golden brown on all sides. Season and cook over low heat for 25 minutes, stirring occasionally.
2. Add lemon juice and pomegranate juice and cook for another 10 minutes, stirring occasionally.
3. Serve hot with fried mushrooms and potatoes.

Fried Chicken Breasts

Kotaa al dajaj bil kaek

You can prepare this recipe and freeze. Defrost and fry before serving.

Serves: 4
Preparation time: 30 minutes
Cooking time: 1 hour

Ingredients:

5 chicken breasts, boneless and skinless
1 tablespoon salt (as desired)
Flour
1 egg, lightly beaten with a dash of salt and white pepper
1 cup fine breadcrumbs
Vegetable oil

Steps:

1. Pound chicken breasts till thin.
2. Dip consecutively in flour, egg and breadcrumbs. Chill for 45 minutes.
3. Deep fry in hot oil till golden and tender.
4. Serve hot with french fries.

Chicken Kabab

Kabab dajaj

Ground chicken dipped in beaten eggs and coated with breadcrumbs is the best meal you can offer to young and old people.

Serves: 5

Preparation time: 30 minutes

Cooking time: 30 minutes

Ingredients:

500 g (16 oz) chopped chicken (skinless and
  boneless)
3 cloves garlic, crushed
$1/4$ cup finely chopped onion
1 tablespoon salt (as desired)
$1/2$ cup finely chopped fresh parsley
1 teaspoon ground mixed 7 spices
vegetable oil (for frying)
$1/2$ teaspoon ground black pepper (as desired)
2 eggs, beaten with a dash of white pepper
$1/2$ cup breadcrumbs

Steps:

1. Mix onion, parsley, garlic, and chicken. Add salt, mixed spices, and pepper. Process well in a food processor. Put aside.
2. Add $1/4$ quantity beaten eggs to mixture with $1/4$ cup breadcrumbs. Knead into a firm mixture. Divide into finger shape pieces. Dip in eggs then breadcrumbs.
3. Deep fry in hot oil till golden and tender. Remove with a slotted spoon.
4. Serve hot with salads.

Golden Chicken with Potatoes

Mohamar al batata bil dajaj

A delicious Jordanian dish. It consists of chicken with golden potatoes, coriander, and garlic.

Serves: 4
Preparation time: 20 minutes
Cooking time: 1 hour

Ingredients:

1 kg (32 oz) chicken, cleaned and cut into 4 pieces
1 kg (32 oz) potatoes, peeled and cubed
$1/2$ cup lemon juice
1 medium garlic head, crushed with a dash of salt
$1/4$ cup finely chopped coriander
$1/4$ cup vegetable oil
$1/4$ cup sliced onion
$1/2$ teaspoon ground allspice (as desired)
1 teaspoon salt (as desired)
$1/2$ teaspoon ground cinnamon
$1/4$ teaspoon ground cardamom

Steps:

1. Place chicken pieces in a pot. Cover with water. Add onion, allspice, salt, cinnamon, and cardamom. Cover pot and cook on medium heat for 40 minutes.
2. Remove chicken pieces from pot. Strain stock. Return chicken and stock to pot.
3. Fry potatoes in hot oil until golden. Remove and add to chicken and stock. Bring to a boil for 5 minutes.
4. Fry coriander and garlic in hot oil. Remove and add to chicken in pot. Mix mixture. Remove chicken from pot.
5. Serve hot in a platter. Squeeze over lemon juice.

Moroccan - Style Chicken

Mohammar al dajaj al maghribi

A main meal which is easy to prepare and delicious to eat.

Serves: 3

Preparation time: 30 minutes

Cooking time: 1 hour

Ingredients:

1 Chicken, cleaned and cut into 4 pieces
2 large onions, peeled and sliced
³/₄ cup green olives
¹/₂ cup lemon juice
3 tablespoons olive oil
2 cloves garlic, crushed
4 tablespoons finely chopped coriander
4 tablespoons finely chopped parsley
1 teaspoon ground ginger
¹/₂ teaspoon ground black pepper
¹/₂ teaspoon ground cumin
¹/₂ teaspoon ground turmeric
¹/₂ teaspoon ground cinnamon
1 teaspoon salt (as desired)

Steps:

1. The day before, mix garlic with salt and spices (except turmeric) and oil. Brush chicken pieces with garlic mixture. Put in a deep pot. Place in refrigerator for 1 night.

2. The next day, add parsley, coriander, and turmeric to chicken pieces in pot. Cover with water and bring to a boil on moderate heat.

3. Lower heat. Cover and cook for 40 minutes, stirring occasionally. Reserve stock.

4. Meanwhile, cover the olives with water, bring to a boil, for 5 minutes. Divide into 2 and stone. Add olives, onions, and lemon juice to chicken pieces. Cook for 10 minutes.

5. Remove olives. Place aside. Remove chicken pieces and put in an oven tray. Place in a high heat oven (220°C/450°F) until golden.

6. Boil chicken stock until it thickens and half a cup remains.

7. Place chicken pieces on a platter. Garnish with olives and pour stock over. Serve hot.

Palestinian Msakhan Chicken

Msakhan al dajaj

The best Palestinian recipe. It is known all over the Arab world because it is very delicious.

Serves: 4
Preparation time: 30 minutes
Cooking time: 1 hour

Ingredients:

1 chicken (about 1 kg/32 oz.),
  cleaned and boned
1 teaspoon salt (as desired)
$^1/_2$ teaspoon ground black pepper
a dash of olive oil
$^1/_2$ cup of vegetable oil and butter
  mixture
$^3/_4$ cup roughly chopped onion
3 tablespoons ground sumac
1 large pitta (30 cm diameter),
  opened (makes 2 pieces)

Steps:

1. Rub cleaned chicken inside and out with salt and pepper. Fry in hot oil and butter over medium heat, turn on all sides to brown. Place in a plate.
2. Fry onions in remaining oil mixture. Add sumac, stirring for 2 minutes. Add olive oil and remove mixture. Place 1 pitta piece in a tray, spread in the middle $^1/_2$ quantity of onion mixture, put chicken over onion mixture. Top with remaining onions, cover with the second pitta

piece (face inside part of bread downward). Sprinkle some water on bread.
3. Bake in a moderate heat oven (180°C/350°F) till tender (if pitta starts to burn, cover with aluminum foil).
4. Serve hot with its bread. Cut into several pieces.

Golden Chicken Wings

Jawaneh mohamara

You can serve this dish as an appetizer or a light meal.

Serves: 5 as an appetizer
Preparation time: 10 minutes
Cooking time: 30 minutes

Ingredients:

1 kg (32 oz) chicken wings, cleaned
2 cloves garlic, peeled, crushed with a teaspoon of salt
1 cup fresh coriander, finely chopped (as desired)
1/4 cup lemon juice
2 tablespoons shortening or butter
a dash of white pepper
1 medium onion, finely chopped

Steps:

1. Pass wings over gas fumes to get rid of remaining feathers.
2. Wash wings with soap and water. Drain using a colander.
3. Fry onion with shortening on medium heat till soft. Stir in garlic for 2 minutes.
4. Add wings rubbed with white pepper. Fry wings until golden.
5. Add lemon juice and stir for 1 minute. Stir in coriander. Remove from heat.
6. Serve wings hot accompanied with french fries.

MEATS

At the beginning, man was a hunter and gatherer. He used to hunt animals and eat their meat as a basic nutrient in his daily intake of food. As the years went by, he found out that it is much easier to raise the different kinds of animals he used to hunt near his house. This was the invention of domestication of animals.

Meat is rich in vitamins B6 and B12, as well as iron, zinc, and protein. Beef, lamb, and veal are very much consumed. Several methods are used to preserve meat from bacteria and decay like : refrigerating, freezing, and canning.

Using lean meat whether beef or lamb, can be part of a healthy low cholesterol way of eating. When you prepare meat for cooking, trim off as much fat as possible, rinse under running cold water and drain well.

In this section we offer you a large variety of meat dishes: grilled, fried, and baked. Some dishes are easy to prepare while others are a little bit harder, but deserve the trouble of preparing. We suggest that you try to prepare our different delicious Kibbeh and Chawarma recipes.

Grilled Kibbi Balls

Akras al Kibbi al mashwiya

The Lebanese mountain villages are known for their excelling abilities in preparing this recipe. This doesn't mean that a good cook or you can't prepare it well.

Serves: 10
Preparation time: about 2 hours
Cooking time: about 20 minutes

Ingredients:

1 ½ kg (48 oz) fine burghul (cracked wheat), washed and drained
1 ½ kg (48 oz) lean meat, finely ground for Kibbi
1 large onion, chopped
1 cup cold water
1 teaspoon salt
½ teaspoon ground cinnamon
½ teaspoon ground black pepper

Filling:
750 g (24 oz) minced meat
2 cups finely chopped onion
1 cup coarsely chopped and fried walnuts
½ cup fresh basil, finely chopped
500 g (16 oz) lamb fat, chopped
½ cup shortening or butter
¼ teaspoon salt

Steps:

1. Soak burghul in water for 10 minutes, drain well, then press with your hands to get rid of excess water. Put aside.
2. Process onion and Kibbi meat in a food processor till fine.
3. Mix burghul, salt, black pepper and cinnamon. Process with meat till firm paste.
4. Knead with wet hands (cold water). Cover with a clean cloth. Place in refrigerator for 30 minutes.
5. **Filling**: Fry onion with a dash of salt in shortening till tender. Add minced meat and salt, stirring, till tender. Add walnuts and fat, stir, remove from heat. Add basil. Mix.

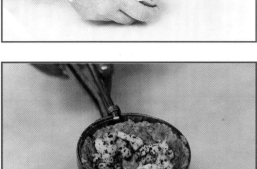

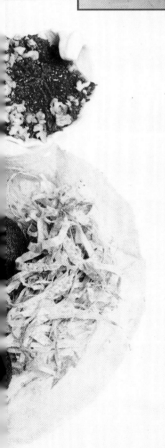

6. Divide meat mixture into balls (egg-size).
7. Place a ball in a large ice cream scoop.
8. Smooth paste into scoop using your wet hands.
9. Place 2 tablespoons of filling mixture in centre of scoop.
10. Smooth another kibbi ball using wet hands. Put over the filling in scoop. Moisten with cold water to seal.
11. Turn the scoop on your hand. Place kibbi ball on a tray. Repeat process with remaining quantity.
12. Brush patties with butter or shortening char-grill till brown on both sides. Place on a platter and serve hot.

Note: You can replace scoop by an overturned plate (12 cm base).

Fried Kibbi Balls

Akras al kibbi al maklieh

A famous Lebanese and Syrian dish loved by every member in the family.

Serves: 7
Preparation time: 1 hour
Cooking time: 30 minutes

Ingredients:

1 kg (32 oz) (5 cups) fine burghul (cracked wheat)
1 kg (32 oz) finely ground lean meat (ask for kibbi meat if available)
1 teaspoon salt
1 large onion
1 cup iced water or ice
$1/2$ teaspoon ground cinnamon
$1/2$ teaspoon ground allspice
6 cups vegetable oil (for deep fry)

Filling:
500 g (16 oz) minced meat
2 tablespoons shortening or butter
5 medium onions, finely chopped
1 cup fried pine nuts
$1/2$ teaspoon ground black pepper
$1/4$ teaspoon salt
a dash of ground cinnamon
a dash of ground allspice

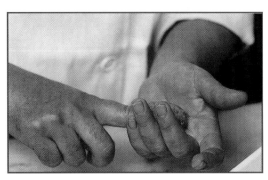

Steps:

1. Wash burghul under running water then soak in water for about 10 minutes. Drain then press to remove moisture as much as possible.
2. Mash onion in the food processor then add minced meat in batches. Remove and place aside.
3. Mix meat mixture with burghul, salt, allspice, and cinnamon. Process well in batches into a firm paste.
4. Knead mixture with wet hands into a smooth paste. Put in refrigerator for 30 minutes covered with a piece of wet texture.
5. **Filling**: Fry chopped onion with a dash of salt in shortening until transparent. Add minced meat, salt and spices to onions and fry until cooked. Mix in pine nuts. Put the filling aside.

6. Divide paste into balls (size of an egg). Dip your hands in cold water then roll each ball between the palms of your hands until smooth.
7. Make a hole in the middle with your forefinger.
8. Work finger round in the hole until you have a shell of even thickness.
9. Fill hole with filling mixture and close opening.
10. Moisten with cold water to seal well and to shape with two pointed sides. If any breaks appear in shell, close with wet fingers.
11. Place the balls on a tray. Heat oil in a pan then fry till brown evenly and cooked.
12. Serve kibbi hot with salads and yoghurt.

Note: you can use a special machine to form kibbi balls.

Kabab Fingers

Asabih Kabab

Kabab fingers are made of parsley, onion, and bread.

Serves: 3
Preparation time: 15 minutes
Cooking time: 15 minutes

Ingredients:

500 g (16 oz) finely minced lean meat
2 tablespoons chopped fresh parsley
1 medium grated onion
2 tablespoons shortening or butter
1 teaspoon salt
1/2 teaspoon ground sweet pepper

Steps:

1. Blend meat, parsley, grated onion, salt, and pepper.
2. Divide meat mixture into equal pieces as big as a walnut. Make from each piece a finger shape piece.
3. Fry fingers with shortening until golden brown evenly.
4. Serve hot with salad or yoghurt.

Note: If you want, grill the fingers.

Kibbi Balls with Shawarma

Akras al Kibbeh bil shawarma

A new exotic dish perfect for parties.

Serves: 7
Preparation time: 1 hour 30 minutes
Cooking time: 30 minutes

Ingredients:

1 kg (32 oz) finely ground lean meat
1 kg (32 oz) ground burghul (cracked wheat),
  washed and drained
1 teaspoon salt
1 cup iced water
1/2 teaspoon ground cinnamon
1/2 teaspoon ground black pepper
6 cups vegetable oil
1 large peeled onion

Shawarma filling:
1 kg (32 oz) fillets cut into strips (7 cm length, 3
  cm thickness)
200 g (7 oz) finely minced fat
2 large onions, peeled and sliced
1/4 cup vegetable oil
1/2 cup vinegar
1/2 tablespoon salt (as desired)
1 tablespoon ground 7 spices for Shawarma
  (Lebanese spice)
a dash of ground mastic
1 teaspoon ground nutmeg
1 teaspoon cardamom pods

Steps:

1. Prepare large Kibbi balls (15 cm long) without preparing the filling (see p.156). Fry them without filling.
2. Prepare shawarma (see p. 166).
3. Slit kibbeh balls lengthwise on one side, fill with 2 tablespoons Shawarma.
4. Serve hot with Tabbouleh and Hummus bi-tahini.

Roasted Lamb

Oozi (kharuf mahchi)

Oozi is perfect for big banquets and weddings.

Serves: 20

Preparation time: 1 $^1/_2$ hours

Cooking time: 5 hours

Ingredients:

12-14 kg (348 - 488 oz) small lamb (cleaned from inside)
2 kg (64 oz) minced meat
12 cups long grain rice, washed and drained
24 cups water
1 tablespoon salt (as desired)
1 $^1/_2$ cups blanched and flaked, fried almonds
$^1/_2$ cup fried pine nuts
1 $^1/_2$ cups blanched, fried pistachio nuts
1 tablespoon ground cinnamon
1 tablespoon ground allspice
1 tablespoon ground black pepper
1 tablespoon ground nutmeg
2 tablespoons ground white pepper
1 tablespoon ground cardamom
1 cup vegetable oil and butter mixture
1 cup shortening or butter (for frying minced meat)
Lemon wedges

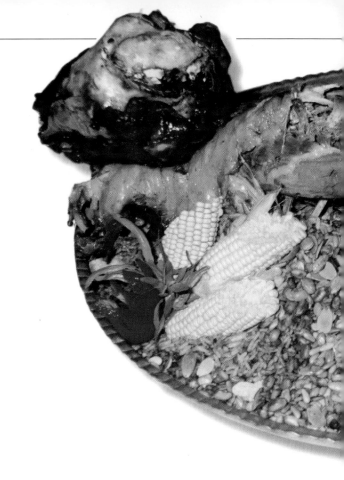

Steps:

1. Fry meat in 1 cup of shortening in a pot. Add salt and spices (except white pepper). Stir on medium heat until cooked.
2. Stir in rice to cooked meat. Add water. Bring to a boil. Cover pot and cook on low heat for 30 minutes.
3. Wipe lamb inside and out with a damp cloth. Rub cavity and outer surface with lemon wedges and white pepper.
4. Stuff lamb with half the quantity of rice. Stitch opening. Fry with oil and butter from all sides until golden.

5. Place aluminum foil on a big tray leaving extra on each side. Place the stuffed lamb on the foil. Pour 3 cups of water over.
6. Truss lamb legs with its shoulders using a firm rope. Wrap lamb generously with the foil.
7. Place the tray in high heat oven (220°C) for 5 hours, or until tender when pierced but still moist inside (add water if foil burns).
8. Remove lamb from oven. Open aluminum foil. Lift up slowly. Place on large serving platter. Arrange rice and meat around it. Garnish rice with pistachio nuts, almonds and pine nuts.
9. Serve hot accompanied with yoghurt and salads.

Meat Balls with Onion

Dawood basha

Originally It is an Turkish dish, perfect for quick and easy meal.

Serves: 5
Preparation time: 30 minutes
Cooking time: 40 minutes

Ingredients:

1 kg (32 oz) finely minced lean meat
1 medium onion, peeled and grated
1 1/2 kg (48 oz) sliced onions
1/4 cup shortening or butter
1 tablespoon salt (as desired)
1 teaspoon ground allspice
2 tablespoons pomegranate thickened juice
a dash of ground cinnamon
a dash of ground dried mint
1 cup water

Steps:

1. Mix well meat with grated onion, salt, cinnamon, and allspice. Divide meat into 2.5 cm diameter balls.
2. Fry onions with shortening and a dash of salt on moderate heat until soft.
3. Add meat balls. Fry on low heat till golden for 10 minutes.
4. Dissolve pomegranate juice in water. Add to meat. Cover and cook for 30 minutes on low heat.
5. Serve hot accompanied by "rice pilaf".

Stuffed Lamb Neck

Rakaba mahshiya

A delicious and nutritious main meal, served in special occasions.

Serves: 5
Preparation time: 1 hour 15 minutes
Cooking time: 2 hours 15 minutes

Ingredients:

1 lamb neck (2 kg / 64 oz), boned and cleaned
2 cups long rice, washed
300 g (10 oz) minced meat
$^1/_2$ cup shortening or butter
2 teaspoons salt
1 teaspoon ground allspice
1 teaspoon ground cinnamon
3 bay leaves
1 nutmeg
2 cloves
1 cinnamon stalk
2 medium onions, peeled
$^1/_2$ cup fried pine nuts
$^1/_2$ cup peeled and fried almonds
$^1/_4$ cup fried pistachio nuts
4 cups water

Steps:

1. Fry minced meat with half quantity of shortening for 10 minutes on low heat. Stir in rice for 1 minute. Add water and half quantity of salt, cinnamon, and allspice. Cook on low heat for 15 minutes. Remove half quantity of rice. Cook the rest for 15 minutes.
2. Stuff neck with half cooked rice. Stitch. Place in a pot. Add bay leaves, nutmeg, cloves and cinnamon stalk. Cover with water. Cook for 1 hour and 30 minutes.
3. Remove from pot. Brush with half the quantity of shortening. Place in an oven tray. Add spices and onion.
4. Place in a high heat oven (250°C-500°F) for 45 minutes. Turn to brown from all sides.
5. Serve in a large platter with the rest of the rice and meat mixture. Garnish with nuts.

Shawarma

One of the most popular Lebanese dishes, spread out around the world. It is best eaten as a sandwich.

Serves: 5
Preparation: 30 minutes
Cooking time: 1 hour

Ingredients:

1 kg (32 oz) fillets cut into strips (7 cm length 3 cm thickness)
200 g (7 oz) finely minced fat
2 large onions, peeled and sliced
¼ cup vegetable oil
½ cup vinegar
½ tablespoon salt
1 tablespoon ground 7 spices for Shawarma (Lebanese spice)

a dash of ground mastic
1 teaspoon ground nutmeg
1 teaspoon cardamom pods

Steps:

1. Soak sliced meat in 7 spices, salt, cardamom, mastic, nutmeg, vinegar, and oil for one night.
2. Fry fat in a heavy pan on medium heat. When it melts, add meat. Stir until golden. Add onion, cover and leave on low heat for 40 minutes or until tender.
3. Serve Shawarma hot with mint leaves, "taratour" and tomato slices.

Shawarma Sandwich Ingredients:

4 tablespoons cooked hot Shawarma
2 tablespoons finely chopped parsley
2 tablespoons roughly chopped tomato
1 teaspoon finely chopped onion
1 tablespoon chopped pickled cucumber
6 green mint leaves
2 tablespoons taratour (see p.11)
1 small pita bread

Steps:

1. Open a loaf of Arabic bread (pita), spread taratour over the inner side of the bread.
2. Spread Shawarma lengthwise, then sprinkle mint, parsley, tomatoes, onion and pickles over.
3. Roll loaf neatly and serve hot.

Shish Kabab

Lahem mashwi

An Arabian - Style meat skewers.

Serves: 10
Preparation time: 30 minutes
Cooking time: 30 minutes

Ingredients:

2 kg (64 oz) lamb meat, cubed (5 cm)
6 small firm red tomatoes sliced
¹/₂ kg (16 oz) lard, chopped
1 tablespoon vegetable oil
7 small onions, peeled and halved
1 tablespoon salt
1 teaspoon ground allspice
1 teaspoon ground black pepper
1 teaspoon ground cinnamon
2 medium green bell peppers, chopped into medium pieces
¹/₂ cup finely chopped parsley
charcoal

Steps:

1. Mix meat with onion, spices, salt, lard, parsley, and oil. Place in refrigerator for 4 hours tossing occasionally.
2. Meanwhile prepare charcoal. Thread meat, onion, tomatoes, bell peppers onto skewers, alternating the ingredients.
3. Grill over hot coals. Turning several times until tender and browned, about 8 minutes.
4. Serve hot with salads and appetizers.

Note: If you use bamboo skewers, soak in water for 1 hour before using to keep the exposed portions from burning.

Golden Lamb Leg with Vegetables

Fakhda mohammara maa al khodar

This dish is perfect for a special occasion such as a birthday or a wedding anniversary.

Serves: 5
Preparation time: 30 minutes
Cooking time: 4 1/2 hours

Ingredients:

3 kg (96 oz) lamb leg
7 cloves garlic, peeled
1 kg (32 oz) golden baby potatoes, peeled, boiled
1 kg (32 oz) carrots, peeled, chopped, cooked
1 kg (32 oz) string beans, cooked
1 large onion, peeled
3 stalks celery or parsley, chopped
1/2 tablespoon ground black pepper
1/2 tablespoon ground white pepper
1 cinnamon stick
2 bay leaves
1 tablespoon salt
1/2 cup vegetable oil and butter mixture
1/2 tablespoon ground allspice

Steps:

1. Remove the outer thin transparent layer of leg. Rub leg with salt and allspice. Place in refrigerator for 1 night.
2. Fry leg in oil and butter mixture with onion, garlic, celery, some chopped carrots, white pepper and black pepper.
3. Heat oven to (250°C-500°F). Place leg with onion mixture, bay leaves, and cinnamon sticks in a large deep oven tray. Add 1 cup water and wrap with aluminum foil.
4. Lower heat to (200°C-400°F). Keep for 4 hours or until tender.
5. Remove leg from stock. Put aside until cool and can be carved.
6. Carve into lengthwise slices.
7. Drain leg's stock, add 1 tablespoon cornflour. Bring to a boil on medium heat until it thickens.
8. Serve leg garnished with cooked vegetables and pour over hot stock.

Plum Stew

lahem bil Barkuk

A delicious Moroccan dish for those who like sweet and sour.

Serves: 5
Preparation time: 30 minutes
Cooking time: 2 hours 20 minutes

Ingredients:

1 kg (32 oz) lamb meat, cut into medium sized cubes
2 large onions, finely chopped
2 cloves garlic, chopped
1 kg (32 oz) dried plums
1 tablespoon butter
¹/₂ teaspoon ground ginger
¹/₄ cup tomato paste
3 tablespoons olive oil
¹/₂ cup honey
¹/₂ teaspoon ground saffron
1 teaspoon salt
1 tablespoon ground cinnamon
¹/₄ cup toasted sesame seeds
¹/₂ cup blanched almonds, fried

Steps:

1. Soak plums in water for 2 hours then drain. Fry onions in butter in a pot until soft. Add garlic, meat, tomato paste, oil, saffron, salt and ginger. Turn to mix. Cover the mixture with water (about one liter). Cover pot. Leave it over medium heat for 2 hours or till meat is tender.
2. Add plums. Cook for 20 minutes then add honey and cinnamon. Boil for 10 minutes till it thickens.
3. Arrange plums around meat in a platter. Garnish with almonds and sesame seeds.

Lamb Leg with Truffles
Fakhda maa al kamaa

A main and nutritious dish served in special occasions.

Serves: 5

Preparation time: 30 minutes

Cooking time: 3 hours 30 minutes

Ingredients:

1 kg (32 oz) frozen truffles
3 kg (96 oz) lamb leg
1 tablespoon salt (as desired)
¹/₂ tablespoon ground black pepper
¹/₂ tablespoon ground white pepper
a dash of ground allspice
a dash of ground cinnamon
1 medium onion, peeled and finely chopped
2 medium onions, peeled
3 stalks celery or parsley, chopped
3 bay leaves
1 tablespoon cornflour dissolved in ¹/₄ cup water
2 liters water
¹/₂ cup vegetable oil and butter (or shortening)
mixture

Steps:

1. Remove the outer thin transparent layer of leg. Rub leg with salt, allspice, and white pepper. Place in refrigerator for 1 night.

2. Fry in oil and butter with 2 onions, cinnamon, and black pepper.

3. Cover with water. Add celery, bay leaves. Cover pot and cook on medium heat for 3 hours or until tender.

4. Place frozen truffles in boiling water for minutes. Remove and place in cold water for 15 minutes.

5. Peel using a sharp knife. Cover with water. Add a dash of salt. Bring to a boil for 1 minute to be sure truffles are clean.

6. Slice truffles. Sauté chopped onion with some shortening. Stir in truffles slices for 7 minutes.

7. Remove half the quantity of leg's stock. Strain. Add cornflour dissolved in water to stock. Bring to a boil on medium heat until it thickens. Add fried onion and truffles to stock. Cook for 10 minutes.

8. Serve leg with truffle's sauce accompanied with brown rice.

Baked Kibbi

Kibbi bil sanieh

Kibbi is the number one main meal or appetizer in the Levant. Whether cooked, fried, grilled, or raw it is delicious. When you taste it you'll ask for more.

Serves: 10

Preparation time: 2 hours

Cooking time: 30 minutes

Ingredients:

¹/₂ kg (16 oz) ground lean meat
¹/₂ kg (16 oz) (2 ¹/₂ cups) burghul smooth cracked wheat, washed
¹/₂ teaspoon ground allspice (as desired)
¹/₂ teaspoon ground cinnamon
1 teaspoon salt
¹/₂ cup finely chopped onion
¹/₂ cup vegetable oil and butter mixture
¹/₄ cup shortening, or butter (for greasing oven tray)
Filling:
1 cup finely chopped onion
¹/₂ kg (16 oz) minced meat
1 cup shortening or butter
1 teaspoon salt
¹/₂ teaspoon ground allspice
a dash of black pepper
1 cup fried pine nuts

Steps:

1. **Filling**: Sauté onion with shortening over medium heat. Stir in meat, salt, and spices. Cook for 15 minutes till tender. Remove from heat. Mix in pine nuts.
2. Drain Burghul using a sieve, then press to remove excess water as much as possible.
   Process twice: meat and onion using a food processor. Remove meat mixture. Knead meat and burghul with your hands. Process meat mixture another time in the food processor. Remove, add salt and spices. Knead another time with wet palms (use cold water).
3. Divide meat mixture into two, make from each 4 balls.
4. Flatten each ball between your wet palms (use cold water). Place the 4 flattened balls in a greased oven tray (40x50 cm). Spread the 4 balls evenly using your wet palms (about 3 cm thick).
5. Spread filling over meat as steps 5,6. Cover filling with rest of the meat mixture repeating the same procedure as steps 3-4.
6. Run a knife blade around edge of tray, then score deeply into diamond shapes. Pour oil and shortening over top.
7. Bake in a moderate heat oven (200ºC-400ºF) for 30 minutes. Serve hot with salads and appetizers.

Kibbi Balls with Sesame Paste

Kibbi arnabiye

A very special Lebanese main meal.
Nutritious and delicious.

Serves: 7
Preparation time: 1 hour 30 minutes
Cooking time: 1 hour

Ingredients:

1 kg (32 oz) kibbi balls (size 10 cm each see p. 158), baked for 10 minutes
3 cups sesame paste
1 kg (32 oz) roughly chopped onion
1 kg (32 oz) fresh orange juice, strained
¹/₂ kg (16 oz) fresh tangerine juice, strained
¹/₂ kg (16 oz) lemon juice, strained
1 kg (32 oz) Seville orange, strained
1 teaspoon pomegranate thickened juice
1 tablespoon vinegar
¹/₂ cup vegetable oil
1 tablespoon olive oil
1 liter water
1 tablespoon salt (as desired)

Steps:

1. Put sesame paste in a large pot, add all juices (except pomegranate), olive oil, and water gradually. Don't stop stirring as you add liquids. When mixture is consistent, add salt and pomegranate juice. Stir.
2. Fry onions in oil then grind in a food grinder. Add to mixture and stir well over medium heat for 30 minutes or till you see sesame paste oil appears on top of mixture.
3. Add kibbi balls one by one. Let mixture boil for 5 minutes. Serve hot with rice.

Note: You can buy canned unsweetened juices.

Kibbi Balls in Yoghurt

Kibbi bi laban

Yoghurt has been consumed in the Middle East for centuries, making it the most ancient food known. This recipe is a combination of Kibbi and Yoghurt.

Serves: 10

Preparation time: 1 hour 30 minutes

Cooking time:1 hour

Ingredients:

500 g (16 oz) lean beef or lamb, finely ground
2 $^1/_2$ cups fine burghul (cracked wheat)
1 medium onion, finely chopped
1 teaspoon salt
$^1/_4$ teaspoon ground black pepper
cold water for kneading
$^1/_2$ teaspoon ground allspice
$^1/_2$ teaspoon ground cinnamon
Filling:
500 g (16 oz) minced meat
1 large onion, finely chopped
1 teaspoon salt
$^1/_4$ cup fried pine nuts
$^1/_4$ teaspoon ground black pepper
Yoghurt mixture:
2 kg (64 oz) yoghurt
2 tablespoons cornflour
1 teaspoon salt
$^1/_4$ cup short grain rice
3 cloves garlic, crushed
1 cup finely chopped fresh coriander
$^1/_4$ cup shortening or butter
1 cup water (for rice)
1 egg, beaten

Steps:

1. Prepare Kibbi balls (see p.158 steps 1-10). Bake in an oven for 10 minutes.
2. Prepare cooked yoghurt (p.13).
3. In the meantime boil rice in water for 25 minutes. Stir in to boiling yoghurt.
4. Add Kibbi balls one by one (don't stir). Cook for 10 minutes over medium heat.
5. Fry garlic and coriander till fragrant. Add to Kibbi mixture. Cook for 3 minutes.
6. Pour in large bowls. Serve hot or cold.

Note: you can fry kibbi balls instead of baking it before adding it to cooked yoghurt.

175

Baked Kafta

Kafta bil sanieh

One of the most famous Lebanese dishes, easy to prepare .

Serves: 5
Preparation time: 30 minutes
Cooking time: 20 minutes

Ingredients:

1 kg (32 oz) ground meat
¹/₄ cup finely minced onion
1 cup finely chopped fresh parsley
1 kg (32 oz) potatoes, peeled and sliced (medium size)
fried round eggplant slices
2 medium onions, peeled and sliced
¹/₂ teaspoon ground cinnamon
¹/₂ teaspoon salt
¹/₂ teaspoon ground allspice
1 kg (32 oz) tomatoes, peeled and sliced
¹/₂ cup shortening or butter
1 cup vegetable oil
2 tablespoons pomegranate thickened juice
1 cup water

Steps:

1. Process minced onion and ground meat in food processor. Knead meat and onion with parsley, spices, and salt. Process meat mixture another time in food processor until smooth. Grease an oven tray (diameter 30 cm).
2. First way: Knead meat mixture another time. Divide meat mixture into balls (as desired) or shape into fingers. Fry in shortening until golden. Arrange in the tray.
   Second way: Spread meat mixture evenly in a greased tray using the palm of your hands. Bake in a moderate heat (180°C-350°F) oven for 7 minutes or until kafta is golden.
3. Fry potatoes in oil until nearly cooked. Arrange onions, eggplant, and potatoes over the meat in the tray.
4. Top with tomato slices. Pour 1 cup of water. Sprinkle salt. Cover and return to oven until kafta is cooked for about 20 minutes.
5. Serve hot accompanied with salads.

Savoury Kibbi Balls

Kibbi Hamees

A Syrian savoury dish, delicious and good for special occasions.

Serves: 5
Preparation time: 30 minutes
Cooking time: 30 minutes

Ingredients:

¹/₂ kg (16 oz) kibbi paste (see p. 156)
2 tablespoons olive oil
¹/₄ cup pomegranate thickened juice
3 tablespoons water
5 cloves garlic crushed with a dash of salt

Filling:
200 g (7 oz) minced meat
1 large onion, finely chopped
2 tablespoons fried pine nuts
a dash of salt
a dash of ground cinnamon
2 tablespoons shortening or butter

Steps:

1. **Filling**: Fry onion with shortening over low heat till tender, add meat and seasoning, turn to mix. When meat is cooked, add pine nuts. Remove from heat.
2. Prepare small kibbi balls (5 cm). Fill with prepared filling. Fry till golden brown and cooked.
3. Place kibbi in a serving plate. Mix pomegranate juice with garlic, water and oil and pour over balls.
4. Serve hot or cold.

Yoghurt with Meat

Moraba al laban (laban amou)

A popular Syrian plate. Ideal for hot summer days.

Serves: 5
Preparation time: 45 minutes
Cooking time: 2 1/2 hours

Ingredients:

1 kg (32 oz) lamb stew meat, cubed
1 kg (32 oz) small onions, peeled
$^1/_2$ cup fried pine nuts
1 tablespoon salt
$^1/_2$ teaspoon ground allspice
3 kg (96 oz) cooked yoghurt (p. 13)

Steps:

1. Place meat cubes in a pot. Add salt, allspice and enough water to cover meat. Bring to a boil over high heat. Remove scum every time it appears. Reduce heat to moderate.
2. Cover pot, and cook for 1 $^1/_2$ hours. Add peeled onions. Continue cooking until meat is tender for about 30 minutes. Remove meat and mince onions with stock in a food processor. Put minced onions in another pot.
3. Place cooked yoghurt over medium heat, stir in onion mixture and salt till it boils.
4. Pour in large bowls and garnish with meat cubes and pine nuts.
5. Serve hot or cold with cooked rice.

FISH

Fish and seafood is one of our most valuable natural resources. It is light, appetizing and nutritious. It is low in fat and cholesterol; it helps with weight control. It can lower blood pressure and reduce the fatty build up on blood vessel walls. Aim to eat fish at least three times a week, including fresh, frozen and canned for variety.

The popularity of fish and seafood has waned in the past due to its unjustified reputation for being difficult to prepare. Nowadays, people know that it needs a little preparation, that is mostly very straight forward and is well worth the effort. And, of course, if you don't want to put in any effort what so ever, try the selection of ready - prepared fresh and frozen fish in local supermarkets (that are growing larger every year).

Cooking fish and seafood is much more simple than many people imagine and it has the added advantage of being quick to cook. The most important point to remember is never to overcook fish and seafood as it quickly loses its lovely tasty juiciness. The best way to treat it, therefore, is to combine it with ingredients and sauces that enhance, rather than mask, this fresh flavor. It is for this reason that stuffed fish dishes are so popular.

The meal appeal of seafood is boundless, and in this section you will find tasty recipes that will satisfy your family's appetites yet be easy and quick to prepare. Many are complete meals in themselves and you won't need to cook extra vegetables unless you specially want them.

These fabulous fish and seafood recipes will show you how appetizing and enjoyable food that is good for you can be. Follow the ideas in our recipes for new and interesting ways to prepare fish.

Fish with Sesame Paste

Aranbiyet al samak

A main and delicious Lebanese dish.

Serves: 7

Preparation time: 1 $^1/_2$ hours

Cooking time: 1 hour

Ingredients:

1 kg (32 oz) fried or grilled fish
3 cups sesame paste
1 kg (32 oz) roughly chopped onion
1 kg (32 oz) fresh orange juice, strained / or canned without sugar
$^1/_2$ kg (16 oz) fresh tangerine juice, strained / or canned without sugar
$^1/_2$ kg (16 oz) lemon juice, strained / or canned without sugar
$^1/_2$ kg (16 oz) Seville orange, strained / or canned without sugar
1 teaspoon pomegranate thickened juice
1 tablespoon vinegar
$^1/_2$ cup vegetable oil
1 tablespoon olive oil
4 cups water
1 tablespoon salt (as desired)
$^1/_4$ cup fried pine nuts

Steps:

1. Add fish pieces into prepared arnabiyeh sauce (p.174). Boil for 5 minutes.
2. Serve garnished with fried pine nuts and a dash of cinnamon.

Fried Sardines

Sardine Makli

For this recipe choose the tiny Sardine (about 4 cms long). Fry well till it becomes crunchy. Enjoy eating it without removing bones.

Serves: 4

Preparation time: 20 minutes

Cooking time: 30 minutes

Ingredients:

1 kg (32 oz) tiny sardines, cleaned
1 tablespoon salt
lemon wedges
1 cup vegetable oil (use another cup if necessary)

Steps:

1. Rub sardines with salt.
2. Put aside for 10 minutes until the salt is absorbed.
3. Fry in hot oil over medium heat, in batches, till brown. Remove with a slotted spoon.
4. Serve hot with lemon wedges.

Fish with Bell Pepper Sauce

Samke harra trabulsiya

A wonderful fish dish from the North of Lebanon.

Serves: 5
Preparation time: 45 minutes
Cooking time: 30 minutes

Ingredients:

1 kg (32 oz) fried or grilled fish, flaked
1 cup finely chopped onion
1 cup finely chopped green bell pepper
1/2 cup finely chopped coriander
1/2 cup ground pine nuts, almonds, and pistachio nuts
3 cups sesame paste sauce (Taratour) (see p 11)
1 tablespoon dried coriander
a dash of ground paprika
1/2 teaspoon ground chili (red pepper)
1/2 teaspoon ground cumin
1/2 cup olive oil
1/2 teaspoon salt

Steps:

1. Fry in hot oil onion, bell pepper, and coriander until soft.
2. Stir in spices, salt, and ground nuts.
3. Pour sesame paste sauce over the mixture, stir constantly on medium heat until the oil's bubbles appears and the mixture thickens.
4. Pour mixture in serving platter. Garnish with fish flakes, lemon wedges, fried pine nuts and some chopped parsley.

Grilled Fish

Al Samak al mashwi

This fish recipe makes an excellent summer lunch.

Serves: 4
Preparation time: 35 minutes
Cooking time: 1 hour

Ingredients:

1 large-sized fish (about 2
  kg/64 oz), cleaned
lemon wedges
$1/4$ teaspoon ground cumin
1 finely chopped leek stalk
$1/4$ cup finely chopped fresh parsley or finely
  chopped celery stalk
$1/2$ cup vegetable oil or olive oil
$1/4$ teaspoon ground white pepper
2 tablespoons salt (as desired)

Steps:

1. Rub fish with salt and spices. Put aside.
2. Mix leek, parsley and lemon wedges. Stuff fish with leek mixture.
3. Pour half quantity of oil on an aluminum foil. Put fish on it. Pour over remaining oil. Wrap completely with foil.
4. Pour some water in an oven tray. Put the fish wrapped with foil on the tray. Place the tray inside a moderate heat oven (200°C/400°F) for 1 hour or until tender. Remove leek mixture.
5. Serve with Taratour or piquant sesame paste sauce.

Piquant Sesame Paste Sauce:

Mix 1 cup sesame paste with 1 cup of water and 1 cup of lemon juice. Fry 1 medium finely chopped onion in oil on medium heat. Stir in 5 crushed cloves garlic and 1 teaspoon dried coriander for 1 minute. Stir in for another 7 minutes, ground walnuts and sesame paste mixture. When it boils, add $1/2$ teaspoon ground red pepper. Cook on low heat until the mixture thickens slightly and you see sesame paste oil appears on top of mixture.

Lebanese Garlic Fish

Samke harra bil al toum wa al kizbara

It is considered the most popular fish recipe in Lebanon. Try it, you will love it.

Serves: 5
Preparation time: 30 minutes
Cooking time: 35 minutes

Ingredients:

1 large fish (about 2 kg/64 oz), cleaned, scaled, rubbed inside and out with salt
¹/₄ cup vegetable oil
2 heads garlic, peeled and sliced
7 cups finely chopped fresh coriander
¹/₂ cup finely chopped onion
¹/₂ cup fried pine nuts
1 tablespoon vinegar
a dash of ground dried coriander
a dash of piquant red pepper
a dash of ground cumin
³/₄ cup lemon juice
salt as desired

Steps:

1. Fry fish in 1 cup hot oil over medium heat till golden on both sides. Reduce heat and fry till tender.
2. Remove bones. Put meat in a platter.
3. Fry chopped onion in ¹/₄ cup oil till soft. Stir in garlic, dry coriander, cumin, pepper and salt.
4. Add lemon juice, vinegar, and some water to onion mixture. Cook until mixture thickens. Stir in for 1 minute green coriander and half the quantity of fish. Remove from heat.
5. Serve in a platter garnished with fried pine nuts and lemon wedges.

184

Fried Fish

Sharaeh al Samak al makli

Fish tastes best when it is fried. What makes difference is the way you fry it and what you serve with it.

Serves: 4
Preparation time: 30 minutes
Cooking time: 30 minutes

Ingredients:

2 kg (64 oz) white fish, cleaned and scaled, cut into fillets
2 cups vegetable oil
1/2 tablespoon salt
2 tablespoons flour (as desired)
lemon wedges, peeled and seeded

Steps:

1. Wipe fish dry and rub from the both sides with salt. Refrigerate for 30 minutes. Coat fish with flour.
2. Heat oil in a pan. Fry fish over medium heat (see that oil covers fish). When golden brown, turn on the other side. Lower heat and fry till tender. Put on absorbent papers.
3. Serve fish hot, garnished with lemon wedges and parsley. Serve accompanied with salads, sesame seed sauce and fried pita pieces.

> *Note: You can fry pita in fish oil till golden-brown, and serve it with any fish dish.*

Moroccan Prawns

Tajen al kamroon

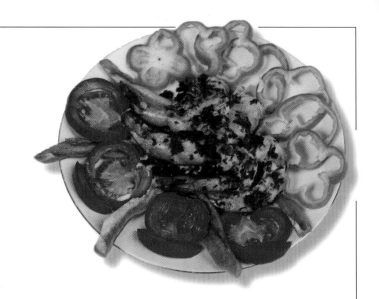

This dish is another exotic Moroccan recipe.

Serves: 4
Preparation time: 40 minutes
Cooking time: 15 minutes

Ingredients:

*1 kg (32 oz) uncooked large prawns, shelled and
  deveined, tails left intact*
5 cloves garlic, crushed with a dash of salt
1 teaspoon ground cumin
1 teaspoon salt
$^1/_4$ teaspoon ground hot red pepper
2 tablespoons butter
1 tablespoon ground sweet red pepper
1 cup finely chopped fresh parsley

Steps:

1. Put butter in a pot over low heat. When hot, fry
   for 1 minute garlic, parsley, peppers, cumin and
   salt. Add prawns and stir for 10 minutes.
2. Serve garnished with green bell pepper and lemon
   wedges.

Boiled Prawns

Al Kraydis al masluk

Prawns are served as an appetizer or a meal.

Serves: 4 appetizer / 3 main meal
Preparation time: 15 minutes
Cooking time: 15 minutes

Ground Fish

Akras al samak bil kaek

Delicious and good for the whole family.

Serves: 4
Preparation time: 1 hour
Cooking time: 15 minutes

Ingredients:

750 g (24 oz) firm white fish fillets, cut into
* strips, each 2x5 cm*
1 teaspoon finely grated lime rind
1 egg, beaten with a dash of ground white pepper
1 teaspoon salt (as desired)
2 teaspoons chopped fresh coriander
vegetable oil for deep frying
¹/₂ cup milk
¹/₂ cup flour
¹/₂ cup dried breadcrumbs

Steps:

1. Place breadcrumbs, coriander, salt, and lime rind in a small bowl and mix to combine.
2. Dip each fillet in milk, then in flour, egg, and finally in breadcrumb mixture.
3. Place fillets on a plate lined with plastic food wrap, cover and chill for at least 30 minutes.
4. Heat oil in a large, deep sauce pan and cook fillets in batches for 2-3 minutes or until golden.
5. Using a slotted spoon remove fillets and drain on absorbent kitchen paper.
6. Serve hot garnished with parsley and lemon wedges.

Ingredients:

1 kg (32 oz) prawns, cleaned
1 teaspoon salt (as desired)
2 litres water
1 tablespoon lemon juice

Steps:

1. Put prawns in boiled salted water. Boil over medium heat for 4 minutes.
2. Add lemon juice and boil for 1 minute. Drain.
3. Serve hot.

Lebanese Fish and Rice

Sayyadiat al samak

Fish is always a great main meal. This recipe is tasty and won't keep you long in the kitchen.

Serves: 6
Preparation time: 30 minutes
Cooking time: 1 hour

Ingredients:

1 fish (1 kg/32 oz), cleaned and fried or grilled, flaked (reserve head)
1 ¹/₂ cups vegetable oil
7 medium onions, roughly chopped
2 teaspoons salt
2 cups long grain rice, washed and drained
5 cups boiled water
1 tablespoon lemon juice
a dash of white pepper and cumin
¹/₂ cup fried pine nuts

Steps:

1. Heat oil in a deep pot. Fry fish's head until golden. Remove from oil.
2. Fry onion until golden in ¹/₂ cup of the oil in which the fish's head has been fried in.
3. Add fish's head, salt, cumin, and pepper to onion. Cover with water. Cook on high heat until it boils. Lower heat to moderate and cook for 30 minutes.
4. Remove the fish's head. Strain stock. Add rice and lemon juice to stock. Bring to a boil.
5. Lower heat and cook for 20 minutes. Serve rice in a platter.
6. Garnish platter with flaked fish and pine nuts.

PICKLES

In the past, people used to preserve food as pickles so that they would eat them through the winter. Nowadays, pickles are served for pleasure and not a necessity. Nevertheless, pickles were and still are very famous all around the world for their delicious and tantalizing flavor.

Almost any kind of fruit or vegetable can be pickled, but they must be as fresh as possible and in good condition. Never use over-ripe fruit or tired vegetables. Water, salt, vinegar, and sugar are essential for making pickles. Beetroot is used to color some vegetables, like cauliflower florets. White vinegar is used to keep the natural color of the vegetables.

Serve pickles as appetizers or as an accompaniment to dishes. We suggest to you to prepare our mixed pickles recipe for surprising your friends or family. Also try the egg-plant pickles, they are wonderful in cold weathers. In this section we have chosen the best pickle dishes to serve your taste.

Green Olives

Al Zaytoun al akhdar al makbous

Perfect with strained yoghurt.

Soaking days: 2 days (changing water twice daily)

Ingredients:

2 kg (64 oz) fresh green olives, washed well,
*   soaked for 2 days (change water twice a day)*
*   and drained*
10 seedless lemon slices
5 cups water
³/₄ cup coarse salt

Black Olives

Al Zaytoun al aswad

Perfect with strained yoghurt and pizza.

Soaking time: 4-5 day in coarse salt

Ingredients:

2 kg (64 oz) black olives, washed and drained
10 seedless lemon slices
200 g (7 oz) coarse salt to rub olives
5 cups water
³/₄ cup coarse salt to dissolve in water

Steps:

1. Dissolve salt in water.
2. Hit each olive separately with a mallet or smooth stone (only the flesh has to be cracked, do not hit too hard as the seed should remain intact).
3. Fill sterilized jars with olives mixed with lemon slices. Strain salted water then add to fill completely. Sprinkle some olive oil over.
4. Close jars tightly. Store in a dry place for 1 month before using.

Note: You can add small fresh chilies to olives in sterilized jars if desired.

Steps:

1. Rub olives with salt, soak in water for 4-5 days. Drain.
2. Dissolve salt in 5 cups of water. Strain, then put olives and arrange the lemon slices between the olive layer in jars and pour strained salted water to cover. Sprinkle some olive oil over.
3. Close sterilized jars tightly and store in a dry place for 1 month before using.

Note: You can add small fresh chilies to olives in sterilized jar (as desired).

Turnip Pickles

Kabees Al lift

Arabs eat pickles with almost all main meals.

Ingredients:

1 kg (32 oz) medium turnips
1 small beetroot
2 tablespoons sugar
¼ cup coarse salt
1 liter water

Steps:

1. Wash turnips well, peel dark spots, slice off thinly top and base parts.
2. Cut turnips and beetroot into slices.
3. Bring the water to a boil then add sugar and salt. Stir till they dissolve. Cool.
4. Place turnip as layers in sterilized jars. Place beetroot between the turnip layers. Add water over till it covers them. Close jars well, leave for 20 days before use.

Mixed Olives with Coriander

Zaytoun mushakal maa al kizbara

One of the many olive mixtures prepared at goodies supermarket.

Ingredients:

½ kg (16 oz) stoned pickled green olives (zayton akhdar makbous)
½ kg (16 oz) stoned pickled black olives (zaytoun aswad makbous)
½ kg (16 oz) coarsely chopped seeded red bell pepper
1 bunch finely chopped green coriander leaves
¼ cup dried coriander seeds
½ cup lemon juice
¼ cup olive oil

Steps:

1. Mix olives, add bell pepper, coriander leaves and seeds, lemon juice, and olive oil.

Mixed Olives with Green Oregano

Zaytoun mushakal maa al zaatar al akhdar

A delicious mixture served with main dishes.

Ingredients:

½ kg (16 oz) stoned pickled green olives (zayton akhdar makbous)
½ kg (16 oz) stoned pickled black olives (zaytoun aswad makbous)
1 cup chopped green oregano
½ cup lemon juice
½ cup olive oil

Steps:

1. Mix all ingredients and place in a serving platter. Sprinkle some olive oil on top.

Eggplant Pickles

Makdous

One of the most famous pickles in the Arab world.

Ingredients:

1 kg (32 oz) baby eggplants
2 heads garlic, peeled and crushed
  with a dash of salt
1 cup ground walnuts
1 tablespoon piquant red pepper,
  chopped
olive oil to cover olives

Steps:

1. Wash eggplants and drain. Cut off stems. Put in a pot, invert a plate on them. Add water, bring to a boil over medium heat.
2. Reduce heat and cook for 25 minutes or till tender. Drain.
3. Mix garlic, walnut, and pepper.
4. Slit eggplants on one side and stuff with garlic mixture. Press to close.
5. Arrange stuffed eggplants in sterilized jars and pour olive oil to cover. Close tightly.
6. Store in a dry place for one month before using.

Mixed Olives with Chili and Walnut

Zaytoun mushakal maa fulayfleh harifeh wa joze
A delicious olive dish for chili lovers.

Ingredients:

$^1/_2$ kg (16 oz) stoned pickled green olives
$^1/_2$ kg (16 oz) stoned pickled black olives
1 cup chopped walnut

Strained Yoghurt Reserve

Labneh makbouseh

Labneh Makbouseh can be preserved in oil for months and keep its taste.

Makes: 1/2 kg (16 oz) strained yoghurt

Ingredients:

1 quantity ($^1/_2$ kg/16 oz) of labneh recipe (p. 13)
3 cups olive oil
2 tablespoons salt (as desired)

Steps:

1. Place labneh in a bowl. Mix well with salt. Make walnut size balls, using a little oil on the palm of hands to prevent sticking. Repeat till all is done.
2. Drop into sterilized jars, cover with oil and seal. Store at room temperature.
3. Leave for 24 hours before you eat from it.

$^1/_2$ kg (16 oz) chopped seeded red chili, fried in some oil
2 tablespoons ground red pepper
1 cup olive oil

Steps:

1. Put $^1/_2$ cup olive oil in a pot on medium heat. Stir in bell pepper and pepper until the liquid evaporates.
2. Remove from heat. Add pepper mixture and $^1/_2$ quantity of walnuts to olives.
3. Serve olive mixture in a serving platter garnished with walnuts and olive oil.

Mixed Pickles

Kabees mshakkal

This dish contains a wide variety of vegetables.

Ingredients:

2 cups peeled and sliced carrots
2 cups sliced cucumbers
2 cups seedless sliced bell peppers
2 cups peeled garlic cloves
10 peeled small onions
2 cups of cauliflower florets
2 cups vinegar
$1/2$ cup coarse salt
8 cups water

Steps:

1. Dissolve salt in water, add vinegar and stir over medium heat. Bring to a boil. Put aside to cool.
2. Arrange mixed vegetables in sterilized jars. Add strained liquid to cover. Sprinkle some olive oil over.
3. Close jars tightly. Store in a dry place for a month before using.

BEVERAGES

Non alcoholic beverages are essential to the Arabic table during breakfast, brunch, lunch, or dinner. They can be refreshing in hot days or warming in cold ones. It could be succulent or digestive. We suggest that you prepare your own beverages using fresh ingredients and selecting seasonal fruits, for a better quality drink.

Our beverages are very nutritious, rich in vitamins, succulent in flavor, and refreshing. In this section you can enjoy hot beverages like almond drinks, or milk drinks, or breakfast drinks: like strawberry drink, or fruit cocktails. Finally the famous Arabic coffee (Turkish or White) is perfect at breakfast or at any time during the day. But, be sure to use the famous small Arabic coffee cups to enjoy the oriental atmosphere.

Always select luxurious and attractive glasses that are suitable to any kind or color of beverages. This will enhance the beverages appearance and make them look more delicious and irresistible. Surprise your friends and enjoy these alcohol free drinks.

Raisin Drink

Sharab al jallab

A special drink usually served in the holy month of Ramadan.

Makes: 6 cups
Preparation time: 30 minutes
Cooking time: 40 minutes
Soaking: 3 days

Ingredients:

¹/₂ kg (16 oz) raisins (seedless)
1 cup sugar
2 medium lemons, peeled and sliced
¹/₄ cup lemon juice
10 cups water

Steps:

1. Grind raisins. Add lemon juice, lemon slices, sugar and water.
2. Place mixture over moderate heat for 20 minutes. Remove from heat. Place aside until cool.
3. Pour in sterilized jar. Refrigerate. Stirring twice a day for 3 days.
4. Strain through a sieve set over a bowl. Serve garnished with pine nuts and pistachio nuts.

Guava Juice

Sharab al guava

A nutritious and delicious juice suitable for summer days.

Serves: 5

Preparation time: 15 minutes

Ingredients:

1 kg (32 oz) guava
¹/₂ cup sugar
1 ¹/₂ cups water

Steps:

1. Wash and peel the guava. Process using a food processor.
2. Stir in sugar and water. Strain well.
3. Serve cold.

Pomegranate Juice

Sharab al ruman

A refreshing juice suitable for summer days.

Serves: 5

Preparation time: 25 minutes

Ingredients:

2 kg (64 oz) sweet pomegranate
1 cup sugar (as desired)
¹/₂ cup water
1 tablespoon rose water or orange blossom water
  (as desired)

Steps:

1. Peel pomegranate. Process pomegranate seeds
   using a food processor. Strain.
2. Stir in sugar, water, and rose water.
3. Serve cold beside sweets.

Banana and Milk Juice

Sharab al haleeb maa al moz

A delicious and easy to prepare juice.

Serves: 5
Preparation time: 10 minutes

Ingredients:

3 bananas
1 cup fresh cold milk
¼ cup strawberry juice
¼ cup sugar or honey (as desired)

Steps:

1. Mash banana in a food processor.
2. Stir in milk, sugar, and strawberry juice.
3. Serve it in the mornings to your children.

Cocktail Drink

Sharab mshakkal

A nutritious drink made from fresh fruits.

Makes about: 4 cups
Preparation time: 15 minutes

Ingredients:

¾ cup fresh strawberry juice
¾ cup mango juice
¾ cup guava or pineapple juice
¾ cup apple juice
2 small bananas, cut each into 8 pieces
4 small peach slices
4 strawberries, washed
4 tablespoons honey
¼ cup fresh milk
¼ cup blanched and ground almonds
¼ cup ground pistachio nuts
4 tablespoons fresh cream
2 pineapple slices, chopped into16 pieces
2 teaspoons sugar (as desired)

Steps:

1. Place strawberry, mango, guava and apple juices in a blender. Blend in milk, honey, sugar, almonds, and pistachio nuts.
2. Prepare 4 cups. Add to each cup 4 pieces of banana, 1 slice of peach, and 4 pieces of pineapple.
3. Pour fruit juices mixture in glasses. Garnish with 1 tablespoon of cream and 1 strawberry.
4. Serve cold.

Liquorice Roots Juice

Sharab aruk al sous

A cold and delicious juice. Perfect for the fasting in the holly month of Ramadan.

Serves: 12
Preparation time: 1 hour

Ingredients:

¹/₂ kg (16 oz) ground liquorice roots
1 teaspoon bicarbonate of soda
15 cups of water
Sugar as (desired)
a piece of muslin
grated ice

Steps:

1. Place ground liquorice in a piece of muslin. Add ¹/₂ quantity of bicarbonate of soda.
2. Pour 4 cups of water in liquorice. Rub well until the color of liquid becomes dark.
3. Add the remaining quantity of bicarbonate of soda. Tie the muslin to form a bag on a bowl.
4. Pour water and turn over the bag from time to time. Place in the refrigerator for 6 to 8 hours.
5. Serve cold sweeted with sugar. Sprinkle on top some grated ice.

Strawberry Juice

Sharab al farawila

A delicious quenching juice for hot summer days.

Serves: 5
Preparation Time: 15 minutes

Ingredients:

1 kg (32 oz) strawberry
1/2 cup sugar (as desired)
1 cup water

Steps:

1. Remove the green stems from the strawberries. Wash well. Drain.
2. Mash strawberries using a food processor. Stir in sugar and water.
3. Serve cold with biscuits.

Hot Almond Drink

Sharab al lawz al sakhen

A hot drink for cold nights.

Makes about: 4 cups
Preparation time: about 10 minutes
Cooking time: 10 minutes

Ingredients:

2 tablespoons clarified butter (shortening)
2 tablespoons flour
1 cup ground almonds
2 1/2 cups milk
2 tablespoons sugar

Steps:

1. Fry flour in clarified butter in a pot over moderate heat.
2. Stir in almonds, milk and sugar, stirring constantly, until it boils.
3. Serve hot.

Turkish Coffee

Kahwa turkiya

Almost every person in the Arab world must have an early cup of Turkish coffee before starting the day.

Serves: 1

Preparation time: 2 minutes

Ingredients:

1 1/4 tiny Arabic coffee cup of water
1/2 teaspoon sugar (according to taste)
1 teaspoonful ground coffee mixed with ground cardamom
(bought with or without cardamom according to taste)

Steps:

1. Put water in a kettle over medium heat, add sugar, coffee and keep stirring till mixture boils.
2. Reduce heat and keep boiling by moving kettle on and off for 1 minute.
3. Serve hot.

White Coffee

Kahwa bayda

This coffee is usually served after heavy meals.

Serves: 1

Preparation time: 2 minutes

Ingredients:

1 Tiny Arabic coffee cup water
1 teaspoon orange flower water
2 cardamom pods
1/2 teaspoon sugar

Steps:

1. Put water in a kettle over medium heat. Add sugar. Stir till dissolved. Add orange flower water and cardamom pods. Boil for 1 minute by moving kettle on and off heat.
2. Serve hot.

GLOSSARY

ALLSPICE

Though it is a spice from the new world, allspice has been adopted in Middle East cooking for its similarity to the combined flavors of clove, cinnamon and nutmeg. Commonly referred to as "bahar".

ALMONDS

ALMONDS are one of the most extensively used nuts in the world. They can be eaten either fresh from the cracked shells or roasted and salted.

ALUMINIUM FOIL

It is a special aluminium paper. Soft and thin used in wrapping cooking. It protects from leaking or burning.

ARTICHOKES

Also known as globe artichokes. The large flower buds of a type of thistle, grown primarily in the Mediterranean. The tightly packed cluster of tough, pointed, prickly leaves conceal tender, gray-green flesh at the vegetable's center heart.

BAKING POWDER

Powder used instead of yeast as a raising agent in baked goods. Baking powder usually comprises two parts acid (cream of tartar) to one part alkali (bicarbonate of soda).

BASIL

Related to the mint family and also known as sweet basil, it has long slender leaves of up to 2.5 cm in length, and tender stems. It is bright green, but turns pale brown when dried.

BAY LEAVES

Whole, dried leaves of the bay laurel tree. Pungent and spicy, they flavor simmered dishes, marinades and pickling mixtures.

BEETROOT

A root vegetable which is a member of the beet family. It is native to the Mediterranean region. The root shape may be globular, cylindrical or conical; the color of the skin is dark purple-red and the foliage above ground is green. Beetroot is usually baked or boiled whole and unpeeled as it loses its red juices if the skin is pierced. It may be eaten hot or cold as a vegetable on its own, as part of a salad or used in soups and savoury dishes.

BICARBONATE OF SODA

Combined with cream of tartar, the foundation of baking powder.
Bicarbonate of soda is an alkali, often used with acids, such as soured milk or buttermilk, to make scones and cakes rise. A pinch of bicarbonate of soda added to the cooking water helps green vegetables to stay good in color.

BROAD BEAN/ FAVA BEAN

The seed of a dwarf climbing plant. Native to Asia. It grows as a long green pod containing pale green, oval-shaped beans which are best eaten when very young as a boiled legume. The broad bean is available in fresh, dried or canned form; the dried bean is cream or pale-brown colored.

BURGHUL

Hulled wheat, steamed until partly cooked, dried then ground. Available in fine and coarse grades. Recipes specify which grade to use. It has a nut-like flavor making it a popular food for those following natural food diets. It is widely used in Lebanon, Syria and neighboring countries. Available at Middle East, Greek and Armenian food stores and specialty food stores.

CABBAGES

The hard, solid cores of green or red cabbages must be cut away before the cabbage can be shredded for cooking.

CARAWAY

Caraway is originally from the countries of temperate Asia, including Iran and Turkey. It has been used as a spice for 5,000 years. A biennial plant, caraway grows up to 60 cm in height with feathery leaves and creamy white flowers. It comes in different forms: dried ground leaves, fresh tap roots, and dried seeds. Purchase from Middle East and Armenian food's stores.

CARDAMOM

(Cardamon, Cardamum)

Native to Asia and South America, Cardamom is the dried fruit of a plant (Elettaria Cardamum) belonging to the ginger family. The pods are cream-colored and the seeds inside are brownish-black. The spice is bitter-sweet, very aromatic and has a slightly Lemony aftertaste. Ground cardamom is widely used in Scandinavian, Eastern and Italian dishes and is also one of the ingredients in curry powder. The seeds are sometimes used whole in pickling spice and marinades.

CARROTS

This popular root vegetable, eaten raw or cooked, is an excellent source of vitamin A and betacarotene, an antioxidant thought to play a role in preventing cancer. For best texture, flavor and nutritional value, buy and cook them fresh.

CASHEW NUTS

The fruit of the pear cashew tree, cultivated in tropical countries and grow profusely in India. The curvaceous cashews have a distinctively mild delicate, slightly sweet flavor and are used in sweet and savoury dishes.

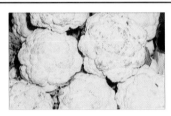

CAULIFLOWER

A vegetable which is a member of the cabbage family. Native to either the eastern Mediterranean or Asia. It consists of a sturdy stalk topped by a closely-packed, fleshy white head of immature flowers fringed with green leaves. A good cauliflower should have a creamy-white head with a firm, tightly packed texture. Cauliflower may be eaten, boiled or steamed, used in vegetable salads or in cooked dishes.

CELERY

A vegetable native to many countries in its wild state. It grows as a cluster of stalks or stems, closely packed at the base to form a heart, opening out in separate stems with leafy tops and fibrous ridges running up and down the outside of each stem.
The natural color of stems and leaves is green.

CHESTNUTS

More starchy and floury than most other nuts and lower in protein and fat. Dried chestnuts are becoming more readily available; these should be soaked overnight before use.

CHICKPEAS

Native to Asia and widely cultivated at the Mediterranean region. The chickpea is a legume which contains only two or three seeds in each pod.
The main use of it is as a dried pulse. The color of the dried chickpeas is light brown and it looks more like a small, knobby nut than a pea or bean, with different kinds varying in size and color. Being both nutritious and flavorful, it is used in many basic dishes in the Middle East.

CINNAMON

A spice native to the Far East, cinnamon is made from the dried bark of an evergreen tree (cinnamo mum zeylanicum) belonging to the Laurel family and is available ground or in sticks (made from quills of rolled bark). Extensively used, cinnamon is said to be the world's most important spice and its sweet, spicy and pungent flavor is pleasing in baked goods, stewed fruits, marinades, and hot winter punches.

CLOVES

Cloves are dried, unopened, dark brown buds. The flavor of the spice is strong, sweet, very aromatic and unmistakable.

COARSE ROCK SALT

Coarse or crystal rock salt can be used in the kitchen or on the table. It can be used for curing foods; rubbing meats and fish with it, is an ancient technique.

CORIANDER (Chinese Parsley)

Fresh coriander (Cariandrum Satirum) looks like unwrinkled leaves of vivid green parsley and is much used in eastern Mediterranean, Asian and Japanese cookery. Dried, ripe seeds of coriander are exported from North Africa, the Balkans and South America. The seeds are relatively small and range in color from white to dark yellow. They are available whole or ground and the flavor resembles grated Lemon peel mixed with sage.

Coriander is used in curry powder and mixed pickling spice. When ground, it also makes a pleasing flavoring for cakes and biscuits.

CORNFLOUR

This fine, powdery flour ground from endosperm of corn - the white heart of the kernel - is used as a neutral - flavored thickening agent. Also known as cornstarch.

COUSCOUS

A North African cereal traditionally served with a lamb stew containing chickpeas. It is made, basically, from semolina which is rubbed between dampened hands to form the tiniest of dumplings, about the size of seed pearls. Although still made by hand in its countries of origin, couscous is now available ready-prepared and packeted.

CUCUMBER

A vegetable (Cucumis Sativus) which is a member of the marrow family and native to Asia. It has been grown in India for over 3,000 years and was introduced to China some 2,000 years ago. The Cucumber is the fruit of a creeping plant and the Western salad variety is tubular in shape, usually narrowing to a short "handle" at the stem end. The Skin of most kinds is thin, green or yellow-green, may be smooth or rough and is generally ridged lengthwise. The flesh is very pale green in color; crisp, refreshing, but very watery. There is a soft central core which may have edible seeds. Different varieties vary in length from a stubby 10 cm /4 inches to well over 30 cm / 12 inches with a diameter of about 4 cm /1 ½ inches. Some types of cucumber are suitable for use in pickles but most are best eaten raw in a salad or on their own. They may also be cooked and used in some recipes.

CUMIN

Middle Eastern spice with a strong, dusky, aromatic flavor, popular in cuisines of its region of origin. Sold either as whole, small, crescent-shaped seeds, or ground.

DANDELION

A plant (Taraxacum Officinale) which grows wild all over Europe and Scandinavia. The leaves can be used in Salads or as a vegetable and the root can be cleaned, dried and roasted and made into a natural coffee substitute without caffeine.

EGGPLANT

Variety of eggplant distinguished by its long, slender form. Asian eggplant generally has a finer flesh fewer seeds than the larger, rounder varieties.

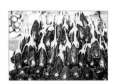

FLOUR, ALL PURPOSE

The most common choice of flour for making pastries and quick breads, this bleached and blended (hard and soft wheat) product is available in all supermarkets.

GARLIC

A herb valued since time immemorial, garlic (Allium sativum) is said to have been given to men building the Egyptian pyramids to keep them healthy. Extensively cultivated world wide and also found wild, the herb is a perennial member of the onion family and grows in bulbs, each containing individually wrapped cloves. The flavor is strong, penetrating and is something of an acquired taste.

GINGER

The rhizome of the tropical ginger plant, which yields a sweet, strong-flavored spice. Whole ginger rhizomes, commonly but mistakenly called roots, may be purchased fresh in a supermarket or vegetable market. Ginger pieces are available crystallized or candied in specialty food shops. Ground, dried ginger is easily found in jars or tins in supermarket spices section.

GOURD

The fruit of trailing plants of the Cucurbita family; many gourds are inedible but the family also includes pumpkin, squash and vegetable marrow varieties.

GROUND CHILIES

Many commonly available chili powders are blends of a number of spices and seasonings, although almost all dried chili can be ground and used as a pure powder. For a home-made mixture, experiment with herbs and spices.

HONEY

The natural, sweet, syrup like substance produced by bees from flower nectar, honey subtley reflects the color, taste and aroma of the blossoms from which it was made. Milder varieties, such as clover and orange blossom, are lighter in color and better suited to general cooking purposes.

Jew's Mallow (MELOKHIA)

A secondary source of jute grown in Egypt and India. In Egypt the younger shoots are harvested and the oval leaves, 4-8 cm (1¹/₂-3 inches) long, are stripped from the long stalks and used as a pot herb for a soup of the same name. The herb has the viscous properties of okra and it is favored more for this then for its flavor. Jew's mallow sometimes makes its appearance in Western city markets during late spring and summer. Strip leaves from stalks, wash well, drain and shred very finely, using about 500g (1 lb) leaves in place of the 1¹/₂ cups dried leaves. Dried jew's mallow is available at Greek and Middle East food stores.

KAHWA , (Turkish Coffee)

In the Middle East every household has its rakwi (long-handled coffee pot). To impress your Arabic host or your guests, know the right coffee talk-*murrah* for sugarless coffee, *mazboutah* for medium sweet and *hilweh* for very sweet. Coffee is always served in tiny, bowl-shaped cups. To each Arabic coffee cup measure of water, add a level teaspoon sugar for medium sweet, a heaped teaspoon for very sweet. Stir sugar in water over heat until dissolved and boiling. Add 1 heaped teaspoon pulverized coffee (usually a dark roasted coffee) for each cup water, stir well and cook until foam rises to the top of the pot. The pot is removed from the heat and the base rapped on a flat surface to reduce foaming. Heat twice more, with raps in between. Pour immediately into the cups. To flavor the coffee, cardamom pods are ground with the beans (3 or 4 with each 250g or 8 oz beans). Traditionally few drops of orange blossom water would be added to individual taste.

LEEK

A vegetable which is a member of the onion family. The leek grows as a multi-layered cylinder of tightly packed, curved leaves which open out towards the top. Although the natural color is green, the leek is earthen-up to blanch the stem to a very pale green or off white. Its size is 20-25 cm long, with some of the fibrous green top removed, and about 2.5 cm diameter. When cooked, it is the mildest and sweetest of the onion family and may be eaten on its own or used in savoury dishes.

LEMONS

This citrus fruit is almost unpalatable when raw, but its kitchen uses are many. The juice, flesh and skin are valuable flovouring; the acidic juice can also be used as a cooking agent.

LENTILS

It is a legume which grows as a pod on a branching plant from which the bean is extracted; the bean is then dried and used as a pulse. There are several main types of lentil. The tiny, bright orange variety, often sold as a split lentil, is a brown-skinned bean with the casing removed; it may also be bought in the unskinned state as a brown lentil. Lentils are high in protein, have a pleasant flavor, are easy to purée when cooked and are a popular ingredient in many Mediterranean and Asian dishes.

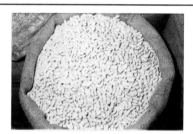

LIMA BEAN/BUTTER BEAN

For export purposes, the bean is dried and used as a pulse. The name "butter bean" is derived from its pale, buttery color although some kinds have a very pale shade of green. All types have the kidney shape. Butter beans have a good texture and flavor and are suited to many savoury dishes. All varieties of butter bean must be boiled briskly for the first 15 minutes of cooking time to destroy harmful toxins found in the outer skin which can prove very dangerous to the human body. Ready-cooked beans are sold in cans.

LOOMI, (Dried Limes)

They are necessary flavor additive to gulf cooking and are also used in Iran and Iraq. While the Gulf cooks use Loomi either whole or powdered, they are only used whole in Iran and Iraq. When using them intact, they must be pierced with a skewer or fork on each side so the cooking liquid can travel through the lime to take the flavor.

MARJORAM

A herb native to Western Asia and to Mediterranean. The gray-green leaves are dried and are slightly aromatic with minty overtones.

MINT

These herbs grow in temperate zones of the world and bear deep green leaves with an unmistakable strong and tangy scent and flavor.

MISTICHA / MASTIC, Arabic: (Mistiki)

Misticha is a resin from a small ever green tree, with most of the world's supply coming from the Greek island of Chios. From ancient times it has been used as a chewing gum. The powdered resin is used to flavor sweet breads. In Egypt a small piece of misticha is often added to boiling chicken to remove unwanted flavors.

MUSHROOMS

Wild, cultivated or dried, the mushroom is a versatile and flavorsome ingredient. Mushroom take well to most cooking methods : sautéing, braising, baking and microwaving. They are also delicious uncooked. We used mainly button mushroom in our recipes.

NUTMEG

Popular baking spice that is the hard pit of the fruit of the nutmeg tree. May be brought already ground or, for fresher flavor, whole.

OKRA

Also called ladies' fingers and gumbo. Native to Africa, it is an angular pod tapering to a point. Young okra are preferred. The vegetable has viscous properties, and while it is used for these properties in western cooking, the preparation of the vegetable in the Middle East is so devised that these properties are lessened. If you like the glutinous texture, then do not use the vinegar treatment, though a brief blanching will firm the vegetable. Okra is also available dried, canned and frozen.

OLIVES

BLACK OLIVES: Through the Mediterranean, black olives are cured in various combinations of salt, seasonings, brines, vinegars and oils to produce a range of pungently flavored results. Good-quality cured olives are available in ethnic delicatessens, specialty-food shops and well-stocked supermarkets.

GREEN OLIVES: Olives pickled in their unripened, green state and cured in brine-sometimes with seasonings, vinegar's and oil-to produce results generally more sharp tasting than ripe black olives. Sold in ethnic delicatessens, specialty-food shops and well-stocked supermarkets.

OLIVE OIL

A golden-green oil with a rich and fruity flavor. The best is known as virgin oil and comes from the first pressings of small, ripe black olives from Mediterranean and Balkan countries. In Latin countries, it is used for general cooking and frying purposes; in other areas, it is generally reserved for salad dressings and mayonnaise. The oil is a good source of mono saturated fatty acids.

ONIONS

Finely chopped, sliced or whole, the onion is one of the most useful vegetable flavorings available to the cook. Native to Asia, it has been a kitchen ingredient for thousands of years. Types of onions used: Yellow onions, spring onions. Yellow onion is strong in taste and available year round. Spring onion should have firm bulb and green stem.

ORANGE BLOSSOM WATER

A fragrant liquid distilled from orange blossoms and used to flavor syrups and pastries. Available at Middle East and Greek food stores. Chemists (druggists) sell a concentrated essence; if this is all you can obtain, use in drops rather than the teaspoon or tablespoon measures given.

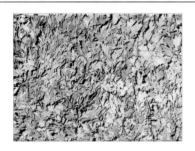

PARSLEY

A nutritious herb, packed with trace elements and vitamins. There are two main types in common use: curly (Petroselinum Crispum) and Flat-leafed (P. sativum), which has a superior flavor. There is also a third type which has a fern-like appearance. Parsley grows worldwide and is used both in cooking and as a garnish. It is bright green when fresh but turns a greenish-brown when dried.

PASTRY- FILO Pastry

Tissue-thin sheets of flour-and-water pastry used throughout the Middle East as crisp wrappers for savory or sweet fillings. Usually found in the supermarket frozen-food section, or purchased fresh in Middle Eastern delicatessens; defrost frozen filo thoroughly before use. The fragile sheets, which generally measure 25 by 35 cm, must be separated and handled carefully to avoid tearing. As you work with the filo, keep the unused sheets covered with a lightly dampened towel to keep them from drying out.

PEAS (Garden Pea)

A vegetable (Pisum Sativum) which grows as the fruit of a climbing plant, possibly native to northern India. It is now cultivated worldwide except in tropical and sub-tropical regions. Peas grow in an elongated flat pod or shell which becomes tabular in shape as the peas inside swell and mature. Both pod and pea are green in color and the pod has a thin, fibrous, inedible lining. There are many varieties and all are sweet and best when the pea itself is relatively small. Most pea pods are sold at 7.5-10 cm/3-4 inches long and about 1 cm/1/2 inch wide. Fresh young peas may be eaten raw by themselves or in a salad, lightly boiled or used in cooked dishes; older peas should be cooked. The pods of some varieties such as mange-tout do not have an inedible lining and these are picked before the pea seed has developed, to be eaten whole and unshelled. Peas are particularly well-suited to freezing and are also processed and sold in cans. Dried peas are available as pulses in the form of whole green peas and as yellow or green split peas.

PEPPER

Pepper, the most common of all savory spices, is best purchased as whole pepper corns, to be ground in a pepper mill or coarsely crushed as needed.
BLACK PEPPER : Pungent black pepper corns derive from slightly underripe pepper berries, whose hulls oxidize as they dry.
WHITE PEPPER : Milder white pepper corns come from fully ripened berries, with the husks removed before drying.

PINE NUTS

Small, ivory-colored seeds extracted from the cones of a species of pine tree, with a rich, slightly resinous flavor.

PISTACHIO NUT

Native to Syria, these are also grown in other areas of the Middle East, Italy and the USA Peridot green in color and uniquely bright, the nuts have a subtle taste and aroma and are related to the cashew family. They are the seeds of fruit grown on a small tree and have pale, creamy-colored shells which split naturally at one end. They are expensive and generally available roasted and salted, still in their shells. They have many culinary applications and need blanching to remove their skins.

POMEGRANATE THICKENED JUICE

To juice the fruit, place a handful of seeds at a time in a muslin bag and squeeze juice into a bowl. Freeze in ice-cube trays, then pack cubes in plastic bags and store in freezer. If fresh pomegranate juice is not available, use pomegranate molasses or syrup, *dibs roman*, available at Middle East food stores. Use 3-4 teaspoons *dibs roman* in 1 cup water for 1 cup pomegranate juice.

PURSLANE

A herb-type plant (Portulaca oleracea) which probably originated in Asia and is found both wild and cultivated in many parts of the world. It has green, fleshy leaves which, when young, are suitable for use in salads. The flavor is mild but sharply distinctive and the texture is slightly sticky. Purslane is also used as a flavoring and can be dried.

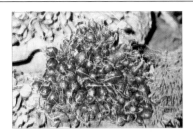

RADISH

Native to southern Asia. There are many varieties of radishes, but we used red redishes. Crisp texture, and strong or mild flavor.

RAISINS

Variety of dried grapes, popular as a snack on their own. For baking, use seedless dark raisins or golden raisins (sultanas).

RICE

This cereal lives in a warm, moist climate and is cultivated in parts of North America, Asia, Africa, Australia and Southern Europe. It has a high starch content and is easy to digest. Varieties include long-medium and short grain, polished, Carolina, Basmati, Patna, Risotto, Brown, White, regular-milled, parboiled, ground, flakes, flour and wild.

ROMAINE LETTUCE

Popular variety of lettuce with elongated, pale-green leaves characterized by their crisp texture and slightly pungent flavor. Also called Cos Lettuce.

ROSE WATER

Distilled from fragrant rose petals, rose water is used for both savoury and sweet dishes. As the strength varies according to the quality, when using a new brand add cautiously and taste to judge how much is required. Rose water is available at Middle East and Greek food stores.

SAFFRON, Arabic: Zaaffaran

It is the world's most expensive spice. It takes the stamens almost a quarter million blooms to produce 500g (16 oz) of saffron. The use of saffron originated in Asia Minor in ancient times. Buy a reliable brand as there are cheaper versions sold which are not true saffron. Pound threads in a mortar and soak in liquid specified to bring out the fragrance and color.

SESAME PASTE / TAHINI, (Taheena, Tahina)

A Middle Eastern sesame seed paste similar in consistency to mayonnaise and used in the preparation of *hummus*. Tahina by itself is spooned on to small plates in the same way as *hummus*, garnished with a sprinkle of olive oil, black olives and chopped parsley and eaten with pieces of pitta bread as an appetizer.

SESAME SEED

Pale cream seeds of a plant widely grown in tropical regions. Sesame seeds are oily and highly nutritious and used since ancient times in the Middle East. The seeds are used on breads and cookies and for tahini.

SEVEN SPICES

It is a combination of seven Lebanese spices which can be purchased at any Middle Eastern store.

SEVILLE ORANGE

The fruit of an evergreen tree native to South-East Asia, introduced to the Mediterranean earlier than the sweet orange. Because of its sharpness, it is not eaten as a dessert fruit but used in conserves such as marmalade and also to add piquancy to meat dishes. It is about 7.5 cm/3 inches in slightly darker coarser skin.

SHORTENING

While gee can be used in place of shortening, the flavor is not quite the same. Shortening is butter that has been melted to remove the water and milk solids, leaving pure butterfat, which has a much higher burning point: 180°C (350°F).

1- Melt the butter over low heat without stirring. When completely melted, remove the foam from the surface with a spoon.

2- Slowly pour the melted butter into a bowl leaving the milky solids behind. Alternatively, after skimming, pour through a sieve lined with muslin:

SHRIMP

Fresh, raw shrimp (prawns) are usually sold with heads already removed but the shells intact.

SPINACH

Be sure to wash thoroughly, in several changes of water, to eliminate all dirt and sand.

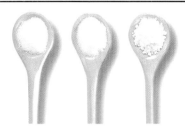

SUGAR

We used coarse granulated table sugar, also known as crystal sugar, unless otherwise specified.

SUMAC

The dried, crushed red berries of a species of sumac tree. It has a pleasant sour taste, rather lemony in flavor. It is advisable that sumac be purchased at Middle East and Armenian food stores.

SWEET PEPPER , Arabic: BIHAR HOLOU

Powdered spice derived from the dried pepper; available in sweet, mild and hot forms. Buy in small quantities from shops with high turnover, to ensure a fresh, flavorful supply.

SWISS CHARD, (Leaf Beat, sea kale Beet)

A vegetable (Beta vulgaris) which is a member of the Beetroot family cultivated for its greenery rather than its root. It grows as a cluster of stalks topped with crinkly, oval leaves which are wide and thick-veined and best harvested before maturity to eliminate stringiness. The leaf is green and its wide stalk is normally white but red varieties do exist. Swiss chard may be cooked and eaten whole but more often the green leaf is stripped off and used separately from the white stalk. The leaf is best steamed, as overcooking destroys the mild, spinach-like flavor.

TARO, Arabic: Kolkas

There are species of colocasia native to tropical Asia and Africa.
It is a large, starchy tuber with side tubers or corns. The taro is toxic if eaten raw; heating destroys the toxicity.

THYME

Fragrant, clean-tasting, small-leafed herb used fresh or dried as a seasoning for poultry, meat, seafood or vegetables.

TOMATOES

The fruit of a branching plant (Lycopersicum esculentum) native to South America. The tomato grows as a hanging fruit, initially green in color, but turning red or yellow with maturity. The size when ripe varies enormously with type and the fruit may be spherical, round with flattened tops and bottoms or pear-shaped. The thin skin encloses a pulpy flesh with a central core of small, soft and edible seeds. Tomato may be eaten raw by itself or in Salads and it is used in numerous cooked dishes where it adds a distinctive flavor. Commercially, tomato is suitable for canning whole or turning into juice.

TOMATO PASTE

A concentrated paste made from Italian plum tomatoes which is widely used in Italian dishes, as well as adding flavor to many soups, sauces, stews and casseroles. It is usually available in tubes or cans.

TRUFFLES

The king of wild mushrooms, truffles have an incomparable flavor. Cost varies from year to year, and prices are prohibitively high. Wild truffles grow underground, around the roots of certain oak trees, and are gathered in the autumn. Black truffles, which look much like small lumps of coal, are most common.

TURMERIC

Pungent, earthy-flavored ground spice that, like saffron, adds a vibrant yellow color to any dish.

TURNIP

Small, creamy white root vegetable, tinged purple or green at its crown, with firm, pungent yet slightly sweet flesh. Generally cooked by boiling, braising or stewing. Choose smaller turnips that feel heavy for their size and firm to the touch.

VEGETABLE OIL

This is an oil obtained from blending a number of oils in various proportions, and types and quantities are not necessarily given on the label. It may contain coconut or palm oils, which are high in saturated fats. Vegetable oil has little aroma or flavor, making it popular as a all-purpose culinary oil.

VINE LEAVES

A familiar and popular wrapping, these have a pleasant lemony tang and are suitable for many cooking methods. Blanching before stuffing is imperative: fresh leaves need their slight bitterness subdued, and leaves packed in brine are very salty. Always adjust the seasoning accordingly when using preserved vine leaves.

VINEGAR

A sharp, sour liquid, containing varying amounts of an acetic acid, produced by fermentation of grapes, cider or malt. Cider vinegar has an acetic acid content of 50-60 %; malt contains a little less, about 50 %. Vinegar is used for pickling, in various sauces and salad dressings, and as a condiment.

WALNUT

It is known from millions of years. It grows mainly in Mediterranean areas. Used extensively in cooking, garnishing and in sweets. The outer layer should be removed then cooked in-order to remove the inner layer. Sauté walnut with oil or butter until golden. It is available in the market: chopped, grounded or flaked.

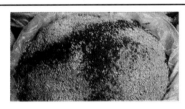

ZA'ATAR SEASONING

Dry blend of roasted sesame seed, wild marjoram, thyme and sumac; available in Arabic specialty shops.

ZUCCHINI (Courgette)

A vegetable (Cucurbita pepo) which is a small variety of the marrow family with a dark green skin. The flesh is crisp and watery and there is a central core of edible seeds. It usually has a milder, sweeter flavor than larger types of marrow. It is best at about 10 cm/4 inches long and may be eaten raw or steamed, boiled, baked or fried. The terms courgette (French) and Zucchini (Italian) are used interchangeably for these varieties of small marrow as there is no English equivalent.